TAKE HEART

A Transatlantic Knitting Journey

❥

FIONA ALICE

POM POM PRESS

LONDON

For my Great Grandmother Alice.

Published in 2015 by the Pom Pom Press

Text and Illustrations © 2015 Fiona Alice

Photographs © 2015 Juju Vail

ISBN: 978-0-9934866-0-9

A catalogue record for this book is available from the British Library.

Editors: Meghan Fernandes & Lydia Gluck

Associate Editor: Amy Collins

Designer: Murray Wyse

Technical Editors: Rachel Atkinson & Jemima Bicknell

Copy Editor: Annie Prime

Models: Natalie Selles & Fiona Alice

Printed in the UK by Park Communications

POM POM PRESS

B203 Lighthouse Space
89A Shacklewell Lane
London E8 2EB
United Kingdom
pompommag.com

We're hopeless romantics here at Pom Pom, in the broadest sense of the phrase. So when Fiona Alice's design submission for our Winter 2013 issue crossed our desk, we were instantly smitten. Her proposal was for a toque (that quintessential Canadian term for a winter beanie) with an all-over cable pattern that resembled hearts. Fiona had beautifully illustrated the story behind the design, recounting a heartfelt tale of adventure far from home, which she hoped would be embodied in this one exquisite hat. Needless to say, we were sold.

When it came time to publish the design, we asked Fiona if we could also publish her design inspiration and lovely drawings - we knew that Pom Pom readers would appreciate this insight as much as we had. We've always believed that handmade objects are imbued with the stories of those who make them.

We continued to work with Fiona, publishing another of her designs in our magazine, and soon after, welcoming her as an intern in our London office. It didn't take long for us to realise that our dream of taking Pom Pom to its next incarnation - books - would do well to start with her. Fiona and her design talents spoke to us as editors; she has an eye for classic knits with a modern twist - the best kind of knitwear in our opinion. She also has a very particular aesthetic; in the designs throughout this book you can see her love of geometry and minimalism, both in her chosen palette and in her use of negative space. Additionally, you will see that the inspiration for and stories behind many of Fiona's designs are all about adventure; her work traces a path across the Atlantic from her hometown in Nova Scotia, to where she now resides in London. So what better person to start Pom Pom's new adventure - the Pom Pom Press - than Fiona?

We think Fiona might have a little of that hopeless romanticism in her, too; after all she willingly came on this book publishing escapade with us! We hope you'll agree that in knits and in life, it pays to venture out beyond your comfort zone, experiment, and share a little more with the world than perhaps you're used to.

Pom On.

Meghan Fernandes & Lydia Gluck
Founders & Editors, Pom Pom

TAKE HEART: *to be encouraged, to be brave.*

In 2013, my first design for Pom Pom Quarterly was published; a toque featuring cables that trace the outline of a heart left slightly unfinished – neither broken nor whole. The name I chose for that pattern was Take Heart. The hat was inspired by my travels abroad which included an exchange semester at the Glasgow School of Art. Take Heart felt like a fitting name at the time as it signified my first extended trip away from my home in Canada and also left me dreaming of ways to return to the UK. In the original design proposal I sent to Pom Pom I wrote that knitting tells a story, and that instead of writing it down with lines of ink, those lines are a piece of yarn. This book is in some ways the end of the story that began with that first design.

In 2014, I built up the courage to seek out a new challenge and began writing to a handful of knitting companies in the UK that I had admired for a while. Pom Pom had recommended Toft's Aran Alpaca for my hat design and I contacted them wondering if they would let me come and learn about their processes. I left home with one suitcase to spend the summer on Toft's alpaca farm in Warwickshire. Most mornings I awoke to sunshine and spent the day learning to crochet, greeting the many visitors who came to spend time with the alpacas or knit in the studio. There were many days when we welcomed newborn crias into the Toft herd. It was a special start to the summer, learning about these gentle animals and the lush fibre they produce.

As the summer was drawing to an end, I took the train down to London to begin my internship with Pom Pom, and was finally able to put faces to names I had been emailing since first submitting the idea for Take Heart. It was an exciting autumn helping out behind the scenes and seeing how each issue is carefully constructed before reaching the hands of their readers. As winter began I decided to stay in London after finishing my internships and find a place in the city where I now felt at home.

This collection was inspired by my newfound transatlantic life. I now find myself travelling back and forth between London and Halifax, Canada, and I continue to be inspired by both the place I grew up and the country I currently call home. In these designs I have explored a variety of geometric shapes and patterns through several knitted textures and techniques. I found myself drawn to classic stitch patterns: you'll find certain techniques are repeated throughout the collection: slipped stitches, ribbing, and large swathes of alternating knits and purls.

After first publishing Take Heart in Pom Pom, I would have never imagined myself working alongside them the following year, let alone living and designing in London. Now, another year later, I find myself publishing my first book. After two years of hard work and personal journey, I feel the term Take Heart returns as an appropriate name to represent this new series.

The last few years have been a wonderful whirlwind, engaging with the knitting communities on both sides of the Atlantic. I'm incredibly grateful to those who have taken the time to help me find my place in London and make this book possible. I hope that Take Heart will inspire other knitters to seek out their own passions, and will find a place in your hearts and wardrobes.

x Fiona Alice

TAKE HEART

Toft Alpaca Aran *from* Warwickshire, England

Take Heart is a fitted toque that begins with a cosy folded brim of twisted ribbing, followed by tangled cables that bloom into hearts, and topped with one of Toft's lighter-than-air, feathery alpaca pom poms. The combination of thick cabled fabric and Toft's Alpaca Aran creates a heavenly winter hat you'll gladly pull on as you head out into the elements.

My semester away from the Nova Scotia College of Art & Design at the Glasgow School of Art allowed me a personal look into the rich textile history in the UK, along with the opportunity to soak up the beauty of the surrounding Highlands. This design grew from my time spent travelling around Scotland and is imbued with the inspiration and confidence I gained during those months away from home.

When I first described my inspiration for its publication in Pom Pom's Winter 2013 issue, I mused that its "...creation tells of someone's inspiration, progress, patience, mistakes and experience gained". I feel these words remain relevant in describing the journey and creation of the ten new knitted accessories that appear in the following pages.

Pattern on page 50.

THREE CLIFFS

John Arbon Textiles Viola *from* North Devon, England

Fellow Canadian and fibre enthusiast Emily Foden collaborated with John Arbon Textiles on the construction of the yarn used in Three Cliffs. And what a yarn it is! The soft merino is irresistibly warm, and each colour is an exquisite heathery blend. It was Emily's article, A Day in Devon, from an early issue of Pom Pom Quarterly that sparked my desire for a new challenge and a change of scenery.

I was hugely inspired by Emily's story of journeying across the Atlantic in search of new opportunities, rather than waiting for them to find her. Thanks to my own knitting adventure in the UK, I am now familiar with the friendly faces of the John Arbon team, and it feels fitting that I should use the very same yarn Emily created, in the country she inspired me to come to.

Three Cliffs is a simple rectangle, long enough to wrap yourself up in, or wide enough to drape loosely around your shoulders. The slipped stitches create a geometric pattern throughout, but leave interesting negative space in the the reverse stocking stitch areas. Although the raised texture is the focus of attention, I think the background is equally important. Reverse stocking stitch is often underestimated, but I chose to have it reflect the pattern in the foreground so as to bring intrigue into the negative space as well. After all, without negative space there would be no patterns.

This scarf is named after Three Cliffs Bay, the location of our first photoshoot. The view from the ruined walls of Pennard Castle, overlooking the bay, is of jagged, pyramid-like rocks jutting out of the sand and surf. The geometric pattern of the scarf is a reflection of this iconic shoreline.

Pattern on page 54.

MARTINIQUE
BEACH

SweetGeorgia Trinity Worsted *from* Vancouver, BC

When I was growing up, I would often visit Martinique Beach on the eastern shore of Nova Scotia, and it remains one of my favourite places. Martinique is the longest sandy beach in the province, where spectacular sunsets stretch along the horizon and seem to go on forever.

I chose SweetGeorgia's irresistible blend of merino, silk and cashmere for this cowl and I love how their hand-dyed, semi-solid yarns add a painterly feel to the colourwork patterning. In my own knitting and wardrobe I tend to go for dark colours and neutrals. It's not that I don't love colour, I do! But bright colours can feel intimidating. I worked with Lydia and Amy at Pom Pom to choose this palette, and was still a little hesitant about the strong, saturated colours when the yarn finally arrived. But I was determined to venture outside of my comfort zone, and now Martinique Beach is one of my favourite pieces in this collection, probably down to the punch of colour. Perhaps it's also because it reminds me of those endless sunsets after long days spent in the sun.

As with many of the patterns in this collection, I've used this cowl as a canvas to explore a series of geometric shapes, this time through highly intense stranded colourwork. The double layers and naturally lush construction of colourwork makes this a hearty cowl to keep the winter winds at bay.

Pattern on page 58.

CHESTER
BASIN

The Border Mill Alpaca Tweed *from* Duns, Scotland

Mittens might just be my favourite accessory to design because they are an essential part of my own winter wardrobe. Creating a hat and mitten set is also a great opportunity to play with the same texture on different scales and body parts. Here the combination of slipped stitches with alternating knits and purls, two of my most beloved textures, creates an incredibly plush fabric.

I discovered The Border Mill's yarn at the Edinburgh Yarn Festival this year, where I happened upon their range of alpaca. I couldn't resist visiting their stand countless times over the weekend to gaze at their colourful shelves. Each shade of their Alpaca Tweed, used here, is dripping with character. There are a lot of heathery blends of alpaca already on the market but I had never seen any quite like The Border Mill's before. Run by John and Juliet Miller in the Scottish Borders, this small-scale mill somehow infuses extra warmth and depth into its yarn. I was immediately drawn to their selection of neutrals and greys and bought several for my own stash, but Night Sky also caught my eye – a rich, dark navy which, on closer inspection, reveals subtle hints of colour. Here I've paired Night Sky with Distressed Oatmeal, a warm soft grey. I wanted a contrast to highlight the two-colour stitch pattern and ultimately bring out the light shades of blue and grey hidden in Night Sky, like glimmers of starry sky on a cloudy night.

This set was named after Chester Basin, a quaint seaside town on the South Shore of Nova Scotia, where I recently celebrated the wedding of my older sister, Mila. The undulating texture and flecks of colour evoke memories of watching whitecaps on the surface of the basin. Bundled up in these enchanting pieces, I hope knitters (and those they knit for) will be able to brave any windy coastline.

Patterns on page 62.

PENNARD
CASTLE

❧

The Uncommon Thread BFL Fingering *from* Brighton, England

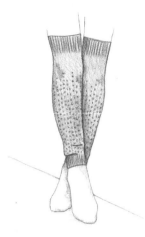

Every Saturday morning my mother and I would travel into the city for my class at Halifax Dance Studio, always followed by a highly anticipated trip to the farmers' market. These legwarmers were inspired by my dancing years, and by the simplicity of alternating knits and purls. They begin with a thick band of ribbing followed by a gradient change of reverse stocking stitch and then a simple broken rib texture.

These legwarmers are exactly what I wish I'd had when I used to dance. They would have been perfect to transition my ballet uniform into an outfit for the market by throwing on a dress after class. Even though I no longer dance, I imagine pulling these on over tights or leggings to carry my summery skirts and dresses into autumn.

When I was looking for yarn for this piece I knew I wanted something sturdy and wearable, but also something with a subtlety of colour to match the understated nature of the design. The Uncommon Thread is a company I long admired from a distance as it is currently not stocked in any yarn shops in Eastern Canada. Seeing the range of colour, hand-dyed by owner Ce Persiano, in person has been a yarn highlight of my time in the UK. It was difficult to choose just one colour from her vast palette, but I managed to settle on these two beautifully muted shades, Tea Smoked and Attic Room, to highlight the different lengths that are possible for this piece. The combination of colours and textures echo the stone ruins of Pennard Castle, the incredible location where we started the photoshoot for this collection. Originally built in the 12th century, then rebuilt in the 13th and 14th using locally mined limestone and reddish sandstone, the colours in the ancient stone walls were surprisingly similar to the colours I chose for the legwarmers. There is nowhere in Nova Scotia that could compare with such a rich historical backdrop.

Patterns on page 68.

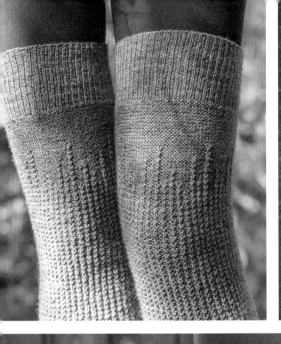

LUNENBURG HARBOUR

Toft Alpaca Fine Sock *from* Warwickshire, England

Lunenburg Harbour is a historical seaside port, located on Nova
Scotia's South Shore. This town is home to some of my favourite shops
and cafes, and is the perfect daytrip destination. After a brisk walk
along the waterfront, these socks would be a treat to pull on once
inside to warm up with a cup of tea.

The idea for these socks originated some time ago; they were the
first piece I designed for this collection, as well as my first ever foray
into sock design. There was no question about working with Toft's yarn
again after their aran alpaca proved to be the perfect match for my
Take Heart toque (page 12).

This time I drew inspiration from a finer weight yarn and chose a
favourite grey to work with. I wanted to combine a delicate style with
the natural fuzzy halo alpaca takes on when worn, allowing it to bloom.
Slipped stitches adorn the toes and cuffs, creating a subtle geometric
pattern, while the double trim of picots and lace add an air of elegance.
These socks inspired the other pieces in this book, and geometric
motifs became a recurring theme throughout the collection.

Pattern on page 72.

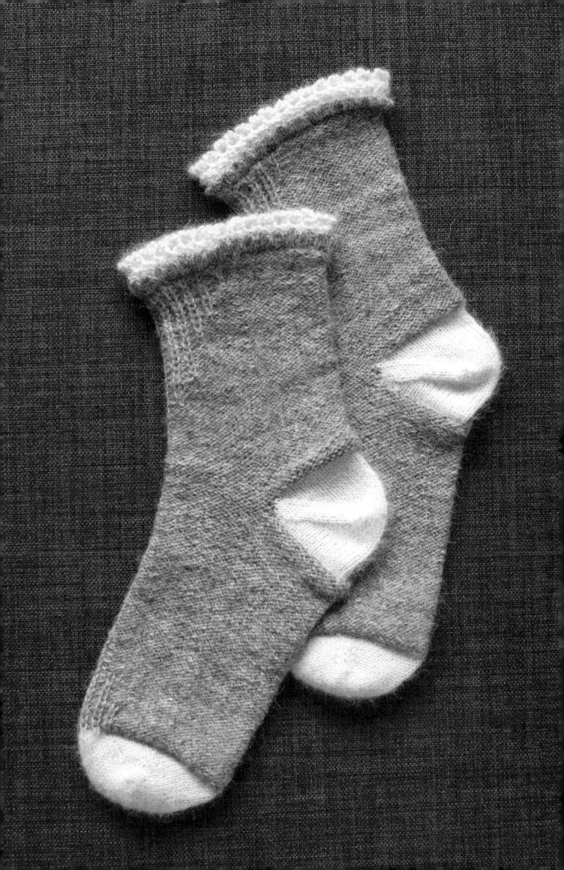

CASWELL
BAY

Handmaiden Fine Yarn Lady Godiva *from* Halifax, Nova Scotia

With a modern cable pattern knit in a glamorous merino and silk blend, this hat and mitten set was the perfect opportunity to play on the geometric theme while also exploring a different technique.
The distinguishing feature of the hat is its pattern of repeating raised geometric shapes against the reverse stocking stitch background, while the other side yields a completely different pattern. I love the look of the twisted ribbing and the way that it allows the hat and fingerless mitts to stretch and conform to the wearer's body.

Handmaiden's Lady Godiva is a perfect balance of silk and merino. The merino provides warmth and structure while the silk adds a luxurious sheen. This Canadian company was my first introduction to hand-dyed yarns when I started knitting. Their Halifax dye studio is not far from the yarn store I worked at, and I saw many skeins of Handmaiden and their sister company, Fleece Artist, come through the door. I always enjoyed introducing their fibre blends to visiting knitters looking to take home a local yarn as a souvenir. I'm overcome with nostalgia every time I use their yarn, as I was when we photographed this set on Caswell Beach in Wales and the sun peered out from behind the clouds, allowing the silk to sing.

Patterns on page 76.

QUEENSLAND
BEACH

—◆—

Illimani Silky Baby Llama *from* Montreal, Quebec

I love designing headbands. They can be that perfect small project for playing with new textures or a quick gift to knit for a friend. Before I started making my patterns available to others, I used to sell my designs ready-made through local boutiques or at my favourite market, Halifax Crafters. I always received a lot of interest in these headbands, but it was ultimately knitters regularly asking me if I sold the instructions that inspired me to publish my designs as patterns.

My Reversible Cable Headband pattern was one of the first designs I sold on Ravelry.com. Queensland Beach uses a variation of the traditional Staghorn Cable and by combining 1x1 ribbing with cables the pattern creates a lush band of fabric to cover your ears.

Speaking of lush, I have a weakness for fibre blends containing alpaca or llama, and Montreal's Illimani has long fuelled this addiction. I love feeling these lustrous fibres slide through my fingers as I work and the warmth and velvety quality of these yarns are perfect for cosy accessories. It was a company I originally discovered during my first stint working in a yarn shop, LK Yarns, nestled in the heart of Halifax's North End, in an area called the Hydrostone. I chose Illimani's silk and baby llama blend for its natural softness and sheen; I love how the hint of silk catches the light and draws attention to the movement of the cables.

Pattern on page 86.

KETCH HARBOUR

Kettle Yarn Co. Islington *from* Hastings, England

The heavy weight of fog is a familiar feeling for those who grow up in the Maritimes of Canada. Ketch Harbour is a shawl to wrap tightly around you as fog rolls in over the ocean to engulf the harbour and shore. When I have experienced fog in the UK it has been comforting; perhaps it's my love for overcast, foggy weather that makes me so fond of greys and neutrals.

It was Kettle Yarn Co's shade Icicle that stopped me in my tracks when choosing a yarn for this project. Icicle's colour, or should I say lack of colour, was mesmerising. The blend of Bluefaced Leicester and silk adds an iridescent quality to this shawl, reminiscent of the harbour it is named after, while maintaining beautiful stitch definition. British Bluefaced Leicester yarns have quickly become a favourite of mine since settling in London.

Like Three Cliffs, this piece plays with negative space, using sections of lace to interrupt the ribbed border. A classic surface of alternating knits and purls make up the majority of the body, while raised lines carve out an image of a whale's tail when you drape it across your back. The whale tail motif emerged as I worked through several sketches before choosing a final design.

The village of Ketch Harbour began as an important fishing community on Nova Scotia's South Shore and remains a popular place for spotting seals and whales in the surrounding waters. I felt that this special piece needed to be photographed against the ocean and am thankful for the dramatic Welsh coastline which made this possible.

Pattern on page 90.

THE PATTERNS

beg	Beginning		patt	Pattern
CDD	Central double decrease: slip 2 stitches together knitwise, knit next stitch, pass 2 slipped stitches over		PM	Place marker
			p	Purl
			p2tog	Purl 2 stitches together
			rep	Repeat
DPN(s)	Double-pointed needle(s)		RH	Right hand
k	Knit		RS	Right side of fabric
k2tog	Knit 2 stitches together		sl	Slip
k3tog	Knit 3 stitches together		SM	Slip marker
kbf	Knit into the back then front of a stitch		ssk	Slip 2 stitches knitwise one at a time, knit together through the back loops
kfb	Knit into the front then back of a stitch		ssp	Slip 2 stitches knitwise one at a time, purl together through the back loops
LH	Left hand			
M1	Work as for M1L		sssk	Slip 3 stitches knitwise one at a time, knit together through the back loops
M1L	Make 1 Left: pick up strand between the two needles from the front to back with the tip of left needle, knit into the back of this stitch			
			St(s)	Stitch(es)
			tbl	Through the back loop
M1R	Make 1 Right: pick up strand between the two needles from back to front with the tip of left needle, knit into the front of this stitch		w&t	Wrap and turn: on the RS, move yarn to front, slip stitch from left needle to right needle, turn. On the WS, move yarn to back, slip stitch from left needle to right needle, move yarn to front, slip stitch back to left needle, turn.
M1P	Make 1 Purlwise: pick up strand between the two needles from the front to back with the tip of left needle, purl into the back of this stitch		WS	Wrong side of fabric
			yo	Yarn over

Sizes: 1 (2)
To fit head up to 53.5 (59) cm / 21 (23)"

Note: The ribbing is very stretchy and fits various sizes. Best worn with 10.5-13.5 cm / 4-5" negative ease.

Yarn: Toft Alpaca Aran (100% British alpaca; 115 m / 125 yds per 100 g skein)
Shade: Silver; 2 (2) skeins

Gauge: 20 sts & 21 rows = 10 cm / 4" over cable pattern on 6.5 mm needles
20 sts & 22 rows = 10 cm / 4" over 1x1 twisted rib on 5.5 mm needles

Needles: 5.5 mm / US 9 circular needle, 40 cm / 16" length
6.5 mm / US 10½ circular needle, 40 cm / 16" length
6.5 mm / US 10½ DPNs for crown shaping
Always use a needle size that will result in the correct gauge after blocking.

Notions: Toft Alpaca fur pom pom in Cream, 1 stitch marker, cable needle, tapestry needle

Notes: For a neat cast-on edge, use a 5.5 mm straight needle to cast on stitches. With 5.5 mm circular needles, knit your first row of twisted rib. Join in the round and continue rib. When weaving in loose ends, make sure to close the small gap in the cast-on edge.

Stitch Glossary

CABLES

1/1 RC: Sl 1 st to cable needle and hold at back, k1 from needle, k1 from cable needle.

2/2 LC: Sl 2 sts to cable needle and hold at front, k2 from needle, k2 from cable needle.

2/2 RC: Sl 2 sts to cable needle and hold at back, k2 from needle, k2 from cable needle.

2/1 LPC: Sl 2 sts to cable needle and hold at front, p1 from needle, k2 from cable needle.

2/1 RPC: Sl 1 st to cable needle and hold at back, k2 from needle, p1 from cable needle.

2/2 LPC: Sl 2 sts to cable needle and hold at front, p2 from needle, k2 from cable needle.

2/2 RPC: Sl 2 sts to cable needle and hold at back, k2 from needle, p2 from cable needle.

2/3 LPC: Sl 2 sts to cable needle and hold at front, p3 from needle, k2 from cable needle.

2/3 RPC: Sl 3 sts to cable needle and hold at back, k2 from needle, p3 from cable needle.

CHART – WRITTEN INSTRUCTIONS

Round 1: 1/1 RC, p5 (6), 2/2 RC, 2/2 LC, p5 (6).

Round 2: K2, p5 (6), k8, p5 (6).

Round 3: 1/1 RC, p3 (4), 2/2 RPC, k4, 2/2 LPC, p3 (4).

Round 4: K2, p3 (4), k2, p2, k4, p2, k2, p3 (4).

Round 5: 1/1 RC, p2 (3), 2/1 RPC, p2, 2/2 RC, p2, 2/1 LPC, p2 (3).

Round 6: K2, p2 (3), k2, p3, k4, p3, k2, p2 (3).

Round 7: 1/1 RC, p2 (3), k2, p3, k4, p3, k2, p2 (3).

Round 8: As round 6.

Round 9: 1/1 RC, p2 (3), 2/3 LPC, 2/2 RC, 2/3 RPC, p2 (3).

Round 10: As round 2.

PATTERN BEGINS

BRIM

Using smaller circular needle, cast on 80 (88) sts.
Join for working in the round being careful not to twist. PM for beg of round.
Round 1: [K1 tbl, p1 tbl] to end.
Round 1 sets 1x1 Twisted Rib.
Work a further 23 rounds in 1x1 Twisted Rib or until band measures 11.25 cm / 4½".

Change to larger circular needles and work Set-up as follows:
Round 1: [K2, p7 (8), k4, p7 (8)] to end.
Round 2: [1/1 RC, p7 (8), k4, p7 (8)] to end.
Round 3: As round 1.
Round 4: [1/1 RC, p7 (8), 2/2 RC, p7 (8)] to end.
Round 5: As round 1.

CABLE PANEL

Working from Chart or Written Instructions, work rounds 1-10 twice (20 rounds in total), repeating Cable Heart Pattern 4 times across the round.
Work rounds 21-22 as given for your size:

Size 1 ONLY
Round 21: [1/1 RC, p5, 2/2 RC, 2/2 LC, p5] to end.
Round 22: [K2, p5, k8, p5] to end.

Size 2 ONLY
Round 21: [1/1 RC, p4, p2tog, 2/2 RC, 2/2 LC, p2tog, p4] to end. *80 sts*
Round 22: [K2, p5, k8, p5] to end.

CROWN SHAPING (BOTH sizes)

Work as follows changing to DPNs when required:
Round 23: [1/1 RC, p1, p2tog, 2/2 RPC, k4, 2/2 LPC, p2tog, p1] to end. *72 sts*
Round 24: [K2, p2, k2, p2, k4, p2, k2, p2] to end.
Round 25: [1/1 RC, p1, 2/1 RPC, p2tog, 2/2 RC, p2tog, 2/1 LPC, p1] to end. *64 sts*
Round 26: [K2, p1, k2, p2, k4, p2, k2, p1] to end.

Round 27: [1/1 RC, p1, sl 2 sts to cable needle and hold in front, p2 from needle, ssk from cable needle, k4, sl 2 sts to cable needle and hold in back, k2tog from needle, p2 from cable needle, p1] to end. *56 sts*

Round 28: [K2, p4, k4, p4] to end.

Round 29: [K2tog, (p2tog) twice, 2/2 RC, (p2tog) twice] to end. *36 sts*

Round 30: [K1, p2tog, k4, p2tog] to end. *28 sts*

Round 31: [K1, p1, ssk, k2tog, p1] to end. *20 sts*

FINISHING

Break yarn leaving a 20 cm / 8" tail. Thread tail through remaining sts, pull tight and secure. Weave in ends, block and leave to dry thoroughly.
Attach pom pom.

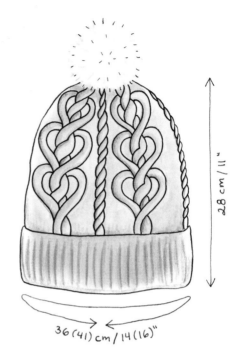

CABLE HEART CHART

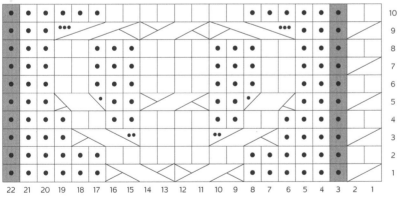

22 21 20 19 18 17 16 15 14 13 12 11 10 9 8 7 6 5 4 3 2 1

KEY

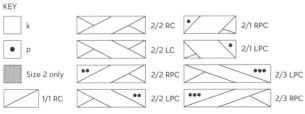

☐ k	⬛ 2/2 RC	◿ 2/1 RPC
● p	⬛ 2/2 LC	◺ 2/1 LPC
▦ Size 2 only	⬛ 2/2 RPC	◿ 2/3 LPC
◹ 1/1 RC	⬛ 2/2 LPC	◺ 2/3 RPC

One size: 38 cm / 14" wide x 224 cm / 88" long

Yarn: John Arbon Textiles Viola (DK weight; 100% merino wool; 250 m / 273 yds per 100 g skein)
Shade: Shepherd's Warning; 4 skeins

Gauge: 20 sts & 25 rows = 10 cm / 4" over stocking stitch after blocking

Needles: 5 mm / US 8 knitting needles
Always use a needle/hook size that will result in the correct gauge after blocking.

Notions: Tapestry needle

PATTERN BEGINS
Note: Work slip sts purlwise with yarn in back.

RIB
Using the long-tail method, cast on 71 sts.
Row 1 (WS): [K1, p1] to last st, k1.
Row 2 (RS): [P1, sl1] to last st, p1.
Rows 1 & 2 set Slip St Rib pattern.
Continue as set working reps of rows 1 & 2,
until piece measures 25.5 cm / 10" from cast-
on edge, ending with a **WS** row.

SECTION A
Row 1 (RS): [P1, sl1] twice, p3, [sl1, p1] to last 6
sts, p2, [sl1, p1] twice.
Row 2 (WS): [K1, p1] twice, k3, [p1, k1] to last
6 sts, k2, [p1, k1] twice.
Rows 3 & 4: Rep rows 1 & 2.
Row 5: [P1, sl1] twice, p5, [sl1, p1] to last 8 sts,
p4, [sl1, p1] twice.
Row 6: [K1, p1] twice, k5, [p1, k1] to last 8 sts,
k4, [p1, k1] twice.
Rows 7 & 8: Rep rows 5 & 6.
Row 9: [P1, sl1] twice, p7, [sl1, p1] to last 10 sts,
p6, [sl1, p1] twice.
Row 10: K1, p1, k7, [p1, k1] to last 10 sts, k6, [p1,
k1] twice.
Rows 11 & 12: Rep rows 9 & 10.
Continue as set replacing a slip stitch column
with a purl stitch on each side of the centre
every 4th row, until only one central slip stitch
column remains. The last four rows will be
worked as follows:
RS rows: [P1, sl1] twice, p31, sl1, p31, [sl1, p1]
twice.
WS rows: [K1, p1] twice, k31, p1, k31, [p1, k1]
twice.

SECTION B
Row 1 (RS): [P1, sl1] twice, p to last 4 sts, [sl1,
p1] twice.
Row 2 (WS): [K1, p1] twice, k to last 4 sts, [p1,
k1] twice.
Rows 3 & 4: Rep rows 1 & 2.
Row 5: [P1, sl1] 3 times, p to last 6 sts, [sl1, p1]
3 times.

Row 6: [K1, p1] 3 times, k to last 6 sts, [p1, k1]
3 times.
Rows 7 & 8: Rep rows 5 & 6.
Row 9: [P1, sl1] 4 times, p to last 8 sts, [sl1, p1]
4 times.
Row 10: [K1, p1] 4 times, k to last 8 sts, [p1, k1]
4 times.
Rows 11 & 12: Rep rows 9 & 10.
Continue as set, adding a slip stitch column
each side of the centre every 4th row, until
the slip stitch rib runs across the panel – you
are working the reverse of Section A. The last
four rows will be worked as follows:
RS rows: [P1, sl1] 17 times, p3, [sl1, p1] 17 times.
WS rows: [K1, p1] 17 times, k3, [p1, k1] 17 times.
Work Section A again.

SECTION C
Next row (RS): [P1, sl1] twice, p to last 4 sts,
[sl1, p1] twice.
Next row (WS): [K1, p1] twice, k to last 4 sts,
[p1, k1] twice.
Rep last two rows twice more.

SECTION D
Row 1 (RS): [P1, sl1] twice, p31, sl1, p to last 4
sts, [sl1, p1] twice.
Row 2 (WS): [K1, p1] twice, k31, p1, k to last 4
sts, [p1, k1] twice.
Rows 3 & 4: Rep rows 1 & 2.
Row 5: [P1, sl1], p29, [sl1, p1] twice, sl1, p to
last 4 sts, [sl1, p1] twice.
Row 6: [K1, p1] twice, k29, [p1, k1] twice, p1, k
to last 4 sts, [p1, k1] twice.
Rows 7 & 8: Rep rows 5 & 6.
Row 9: [P1, sl1] twice, p27, [sl1, p1] 3 times, sl1,
p to last 4 sts, [sl1, p1] twice.
Row 10: [K1, p1] twice, k27, [p1, k1] 3 times, p1,
k to last 4 sts, [p1, k1] twice.
Rows 11 & 12: Rep rows 9 & 10.
Continue working in pattern until there are 17
slip stitch columns. Now stop increasing here
and begin to decrease two slip stitch columns
every 4th row, stopping when there is one
column remaining.
Work Section C again.

SECTION E

Begin working as Section D **but** continue adding two slip stitch columns on each side, every 4th row until last 4 rows read:

RS rows: [P1, sl1] twice, p3, [sl1, p1] rep to last 6 sts, p2, [sl1, p1] twice.

WS rows: [K1, p1] twice, k3, [p1, k1] rep to last 6 sts, k2, [p1, k1] twice.

SECTION F

Row 1 (RS): [P1, sl1] 17 times, p3, [sl1, p1] 17 times.

Row 2 (WS): [K1, p1] 17 times, k3, [p1, k1] 17 times.

Rows 3 & 4: Rep rows 1 & 2.

Row 5: [P1, sl1] 16 times, p7, [sl1, p1] 16 times.

Row 6: [K1, p1] 16 times, k7, [p1, k1] 16 times.

Rows 7 & 8: Rep rows 5 & 6.

Row 9: [P1, sl1] 15 times, p11, [sl1, p1] 15 times.

Row 10: [K1, p1] 15 times, k11, [p1, k1] 15 times.

Rows 11 & 12: Rep rows 9 & 10.

Continue in pattern decreasing two slip stitch columns every 4th row, until last four rows read:

RS rows: [P1, sl1] twice, p to the last 4 sts, [sl1, p1] twice.

WS rows: [K1, p1] twice, k to the last 4 sts, [p1, k1] twice.

Work Section E again.

Work Slip St Rib patt for 25.5 cm / 10", ending with a WS row.

Cast off in pattern.

FINISHING

Weave in ends and block to measurements.

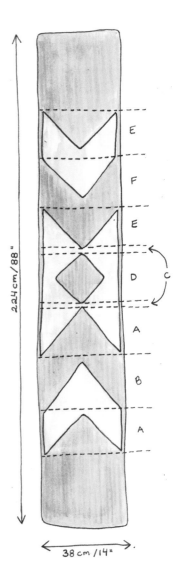

One size: 113 cm / 44½" circumference x 20 cm / 7¾" wide (width measured flat)

Yarn: SweetGeorgia Trinity Worsted (worsted weight; 70% superwash merino wool, 20% cashmere, 10% silk; 183 m / 200 yds per 115 g skein)

Shades:

A: Pumpkin x 1 skein

B: Birch x 1 skein

C: Oxblood x 1 skein

D: Black Plum x 1 skein

Gauge: 20 sts & 21 rows = 10 cm / 4" over colourwork pattern on 5 mm needles after blocking

Needles: 5 mm / US 8 circular needle, 40 cm / 16" length
Additional circular needle in a similar size
5 mm / US H/8 crochet hook for provisional cast-on
Always use a needle size that will result in the correct gauge after blocking.

Notions: Waste yarn in a similar weight for provisional cast on, stitch marker, tapestry needle

PATTERN BEGINS

Using the provisional crochet method, cast
on 80 sts. Join for working in the round being
careful not to twist. PM to indicate beg of
round.

Reading the charts from right to left for every
row, working bottom to top and changing
colours as indicated, work all rows of Chart
A followed by Chart B, Chart C and Chart D.
Now repeat all rows of Chart A, Chart B and
Chart C, then repeat rows 1-23 only of Chart D.

Note: The colourwork charts contain both
8-stitch and 10-stitch repeat sections; When
working a section of 8 sts, repeat that section
10 times across the round, and the 10-stitch
sections 8 times.

Break yarns, leaving an extra long tail of yarn
C. Piece should measure approximately 108
cm / 42½" after knitting – the scarf will grow
slightly in length during blocking.

FINISHING

Weave in ends. Unzip the provisional cast-on
and slip these stitches onto the spare circular
needle. Hold the two ends together so the sts
are parallel to one another, and use the long
yarn C tail to graft the ends together with
Kitchener Stitch.

Soak scarf and block to measurements leaving
to dry thoroughly.

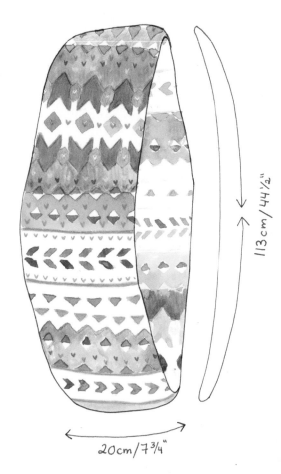

113cm / 44½"

20cm / 7¾"

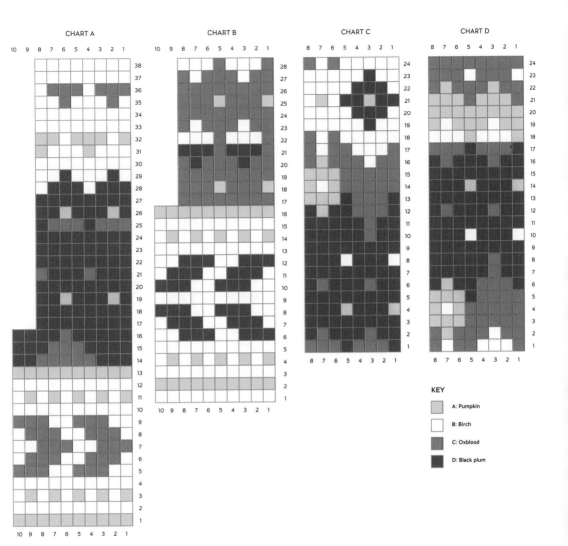

CHART A

CHART B

CHART C

CHART D

KEY

A: Pumpkin

B: Birch

C: Oxblood

D: Black plum

Sizes: 1 (2, 3)

To fit head circumference: 48 (51, 55) cm / 19 (20, 21½)" – to be worn with approximately 5 cm / 2" negative ease

Finished circumference: 43 (46, 50) cm / 17 (18, 19½)"

Finished height with brim folded up: 24 (25.5, 27) cm / 9½ (10, 10½)"

Yarn: The Border Mill Alpaca Tweed (heavy worsted weight; 100% alpaca; 170 m / 186 yds per 100 g skein)

A: Distressed Oatmeal; 1 (1, 1) skein

B: Night Sky; 1 (1, 1) skein

Note: 1 skein of each colour will be sufficient to make both the Border Mill hat and mittens.

Gauge: 22 sts & 54 rows = 10 cm / 4" over Corn on the Cob Pattern on 6 mm needles after blocking

Note: The high row count is due to the slip stitch pattern.

Needles: 4.5 mm / US 7 circular needle, 40 cm / 16" length
6 mm / US 10 circular needle, 40 cm / 16" length
4.5 mm / US 7 DPNs for crown shaping
Always use a needle size that will result in the correct gauge after blocking.

Notions: Stitch marker, tapestry needle
Notes: When working Corn on the Cob
Pattern, do not break yarn between rounds of
yarn B and yarn A – carry them loosely up the
inside of the hat.

CORN ON THE COB PATTERN
Note: Work slip sts purlwise with yarn in back.
Round 1: Using yarn A, [sl1, k1 tbl] to end.
Round 2: Using yarn A, [sl1, p1] to end.
Round 3: Using yarn B, [k1, sl1] to end.
Round 4: Using yarn B, [p1, sl1] to end.
Rep rounds 1-4 for pattern.

PATTERN BEGINS
Using smaller needles, yarn A and the long-
tail method, cast on 90 (100, 110) sts. Join
for working in the round being careful not to
twist. PM to indicate beg of round.

BRIM
Round 1: [K1, p1] to end.
Round 1 sets 1x1 Rib pattern.
Break yarn A, leaving a tail to weave in later.
Join yarn B and work 1x1 Rib until brim
measures 9 cm / 3½" from cast-on edge.
Next round: Knit.

MAIN BODY
Change to larger needles and rejoin yarn A
without breaking yarn B.
Work in Corn on the Cob Pattern until hat
measures 27 (28, 29) cm / 10½ (11, 11½)" from
cast-on edge ending with round 4 of pattern.
Break yarn B, leaving a tail to weave in later,
and continue in yarn A only.
Next round: [Sl1, k1] to end.

CROWN
Change to smaller needles and work crown
shaping as follows, switching to DPNs as
required:
Rounds 1 & 2: Knit.
Round 3: [K3, k2tog] to end. *72 (80, 88) sts*
Round 4: Knit.
Round 5: [K2, k2tog] to end. *54 (60, 66) sts*
Round 6: Knit.

Round 7: [K1, k2tog] to end. *36 (40, 44) sts*
Round 8: Knit.
Round 9: [K2tog] to end. *18 (20, 22) sts*
Round 10: Knit.
Round 11: [K2tog] to end. *9 (10, 11) sts*
Break yarn and thread tail through remaining sts.

FINISHING
Weave in ends and gently block to
measurements laying the hat flat to dry and
taking care not to overstretch the rib.
Finish with an optional pom pom if the mood
takes you!

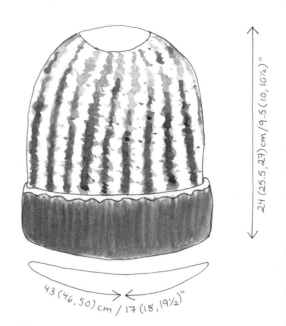

24 (25.5, 27) cm / 9.5 (10, 10½)"

43 (46, 50) cm / 17 (18, 19½)"

Sizes: 1 (2, 3)
Finished circumference: 18 (19, 20) cm / 7 (7½, 8)"
Finished length: 24 (25, 27) cm / 9½ (10, 10½)"

Yarn: The Border Mill Alpaca Tweed (heavy worsted weight; 100% alpaca; 170 m / 186 yds per 100 g skein)
A: Distressed Oatmeal; 1 (1, 1) skein
B: Night Sky; 1 (1, 1) skein
Note: 1 skein of each colour will be sufficient to make both the Chester Basin mittens and hat.

Gauge: 24 sts & 58 rows = 10 cm / 4" over Corn on the Cob Pattern on 5 mm needles after blocking
Note: The high row count is due to the slip stitch pattern.

Needles: 4 mm / US 6 DPNs **or** circular needle, 80 cm / 32" length for magic loop
5 mm / US 8 DPNs **or** circular needle, 80 cm / 32" length for magic loop
Always use a needle size that will result in the correct gauge after blocking.

Notions: 3 stitch markers, stitch holder or waste yarn, tapestry needle

Notes: Whilst the mittens use the same stitch pattern as the Chester Basin Hat, the gauge is tighter to produce a denser fabric more suited to warm mittens.
When working Corn on the Cob Pattern, do not break yarn between rounds of yarn B and yarn A – carry them loosely up the inside of the mitten.

CORN ON THE COB PATTERN
Note: Work slip sts purlwise with yarn in back.
Round 1: Using yarn A, [sl1, k1 tbl] to end.
Round 2: Using yarn A, [sl1, p1] to end.
Round 3: Using yarn B, [k1, sl1] to end.
Round 4: Using yarn B, [p1, sl1] to end.
Rep rounds 1-4 for pattern.

PATTERN BEGINS
(make 2 alike)

Using smaller needles, yarn A and the long-tail method, cast on 32 (36, 40) sts. Join for working in the round being careful not to twist. PM to indicate beg of round.

CUFF
Round 1: [K1, p1] to end.
Round 1 sets 1x1 Rib pattern.
Break yarn A, leaving a tail to weave in later. Join yarn B and work 20 rounds of 1x1 Rib.
Next round: [K4 (4, 5), M1R] 8 times, k0 (4, 0). *40 (44, 48) sts*

MAIN BODY
Change to larger needles and rejoin yarn A without breaking yarn B.
Work 20 (20, 24) rounds in Corn on the Cob Pattern.
Continue in Corn on the Cob Pattern and increase for gusset as follows:
Round 1: Patt 19 (21, 23) sts, yo, PM, patt 3 sts, PM, yo, patt to end. *42 (46, 50) sts*
Round 2: Patt to yo, k1 tbl, SM, patt 3 sts, SM, k1 tbl, patt to end.
Round 3: Patt to marker, yo, SM, patt 3 sts, SM, yo, patt to end. *2 sts inc*
Round 4: Patt to yo, k1 tbl, SM, patt 3 sts, SM, k1 tbl, patt to end.
Rep rounds 3 & 4, increasing 2 sts every other round as set a further 3 (4, 4) times, and taking the increased sts into Corn on the Cob Pattern. *50 (56, 60) sts*
Work 4 rounds of Corn on the Cob Pattern across all sts.
Next round: Patt 19 (21, 23) sts, place next 13 (15, 15) sts on stitch holder or waste yarn for thumb and remove gusset markers, cast 3 sts onto RH needle to close gap, patt to end. *40 (44, 48) sts*
Continue in Corn on the Cob Pattern until mitten measures 23 (24, 25.5) cm / 9 (9½, 10)" from cast-on edge, or until mitten reaches the top of your index finger.

Change to smaller needle, break yarn B
leaving a tail to weave in, and continue in yarn
A only.
Next round: Knit.

MITTEN TOP
Round 1: [K2, k2tog] to end. *30 (33, 36) sts*
Round 2: Knit.
Round 3: [K1, k2tog] to end. *20 (22, 24) sts*
Round 4: Knit.
Round 5: [K2tog] to end. *10 (11, 12) sts*
Break yarn and thread tail through remaining sts.

THUMB
Place the held 13 (15, 15) thumb sts on larger
needles.
Round 1: Working in yarn A only, pick up
and k5 sts across the gap (1 in each of the 3
cast-on sts and 1 each side) then k13 (15, 15)
sts, join for working in the round and PM to
indicate beg of round. *18 (20, 20) sts*
Size 1 ONLY: [K3, k2tog, k2, k2tog] twice. *14 sts*
Sizes 2 & 3 ONLY: [K3, k2tog] 4 times. *16 (16) sts*
ALL sizes again:
Knit 12 (14, 16) rounds, or desired length to tip
of your thumb.
Next round: [K2tog] to end. *7 (8, 8) sts*
Break yarn and thread tail through remaining sts.

FINISHING
Weave in all ends and gently block to
measurements laying flat to dry.

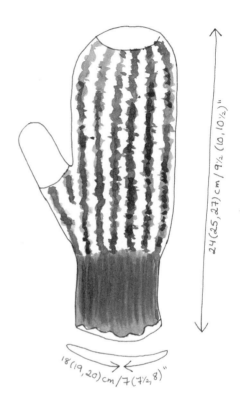

24 (25, 27) cm / 9½ (10, 10½)"

18 (19, 20) cm / 7 (7½, 8)"

Thigh Length Version

Sizes: 1 (2, 3)

To fit thigh circumference: 40.5 (46, 51) cm / 16 (18, 20)" – to be worn with approximately 5 cm / 2" negative ease

Calf Length Version

Sizes: 1 (2, 3)

To fit leg circumference: 30.5 (35.5, 40.5) cm / 12 (14, 16)" – to be worn with approximately 5 cm / 2" negative ease

Models are wearing the smallest size.

Yarn: The Uncommon Thread BFL Fingering (4ply/Fingering weight; 100% superwash Bluefaced Leicester wool; 400 m / 437 yds per 100 g skein)

Thigh Length Version: Attic Room; 2 (2, 3) skeins

Calf Length Version: Tea Smoked 2 (2, 2) skeins

Gauge: 32 sts & 42 rows = 10 cm / 4" over Broken Rib (unstretched) on 3 mm needles after blocking

Needles: 2.5 mm / US 1.5 DPNs **or** circular needle, 80 cm / 32" length for magic loop 3 mm / US 2.5 DPNs **or** circular needle, 80 cm / 32" length for magic loop

Always use a needle size that will result in the correct gauge after blocking.

Notions: Fine elastic thread, tapestry needle

Notes: These legwarmers are worked inside out so that the majority of the stitches are knit instead of purl – ultimately the legwarmers are reversible and can be worn with either texture of the Broken Rib showing. The fine elastic thread and yarn are held together whilst working the band of ribbing at the top of the leg. Hold the elastic taught as you knit it. Using the elastic is highly recommended but not necessary.

Stitch Glossary

1x1 Rib
Every round: [K1, p1] to end.

Broken Rib
Round 1: [K1, p1] to end.
Round 2: Knit.

PATTERN BEGINS – THIGH LENGTH VERSION (make 2 alike)

Using smaller needles and the long-tail method, cast on 112 (126, 140) sts. Join for working in the round being careful not to twist. PM to indicate beg of round.

UPPER CUFF

Holding the elastic with the yarn, work 48 rounds of 1x1 Rib.
Break elastic, leaving a tail to weave in later.
Change to larger needles and knit 15 rounds.

TRANSITION SECTION

Round 1: [K5, p1, k8] to end.
Round 2 & ALL following even-numbered rounds: Knit.
Round 3: As Round 1.
Round 5: [K5, p1, k3, p1, k4] to end.
Round 7: As round 5.
Round 9: [K1, (p1, k3) twice, p1, k4] to end.
Round 11: As round 9.
Round 13: [K1, p1, k3, (p1, k1) twice, p1, k3, p1] to end.
Round 15: As round 13.
Round 16 (even round): Knit. **

BROKEN RIB SECTION

Work Broken Rib for 4 rounds.
Continue in Broken Rib throughout this section as follows:
Note: Broken Rib is now referred to as 'patt'.
Round 1: Patt 27 (31, 34) sts, CDD, patt to end. *110 (124, 138) sts*
Round 2 & ALL following even-numbered rounds: Knit.
Round 3: [K1, p1] to end.

Round 5: Patt 26 (30, 33) sts, CDD, patt to end. *108 (122, 136) sts*

Round 7: [K1, p1] to end.

Round 9: Patt 25 (29, 32) sts, CDD, patt to end. *106 (120, 134) sts*

Round 11: [K1, p1] to end.
Continue working decrease rounds every 4th round as set until 84 (98, 112) sts remain and you have worked 13 decrease rounds in total, ending with a decrease round.
The legwarmer should reach the top of your calf muscle. If you'd like a narrower fit around the leg, work a few more decrease rounds as set.

Work straight in Broken Rib until the legwarmer reaches to approximately 5 cm / 2" **before** your anklebone.
Work second decrease section as follows:
Round 1: Patt 14 (17, 22) sts, CDD, patt to end. *82 (96, 110) sts*

Round 2 & ALL following even-numbered rounds: Knit.

Round 3: [K1, p1] to end of round.

Round 5: Patt 13 (16, 21) sts, CDD, patt to end. *80 (94, 108) sts*

Round 7: [K1, p1] to end of round.
Continue working decrease rounds every 4th round as set until 70 (84, 98) sts remain and you have worked 6 decrease rounds in total, ending with a decrease round.
Knit 1 round.

BOTTOM CUFF

Change to smaller needles and work 1x1 Rib for 10 rounds. If desired you can use the elastic here again.
Cast off loosely in rib.

FINISHING

Weave in ends and turn right side out. Block gently and lay flat to dry. The legwarmers will grow slightly in length after blocking.

PATTERN BEGINS – CALF LENGTH VERSION (make 2 alike)

Using smaller needles and the long-tail method, cast on 84 (98, 112) sts. Join for working in the round being careful not to twist. PM to indicate beg of round.
Work cuff and transition section as for the Thigh Length Version to **.
Work Broken Rib until legwarmer reaches to approximately 5 cm / 2" **before** your anklebone.
Work second decrease section, bottom cuff, cast off and finishing as for Thigh Length version.

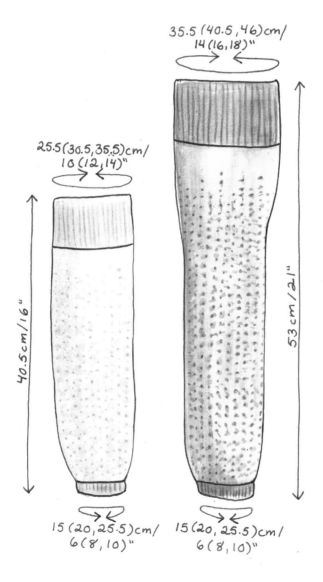

35.5 (40.5, 46) cm/
14 (16, 18)"

25.5 (30.5, 35.5) cm/
10 (12, 14)"

40.5 cm / 16"

53 cm / 21"

15 (20, 25.5) cm/
6 (8, 10)"

15 (20, 25.5) cm/
6 (8, 10)"

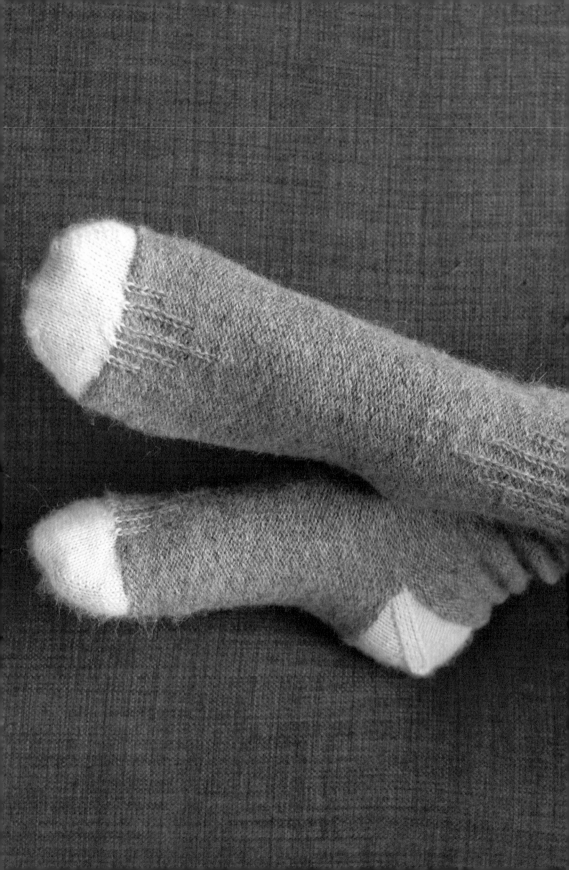

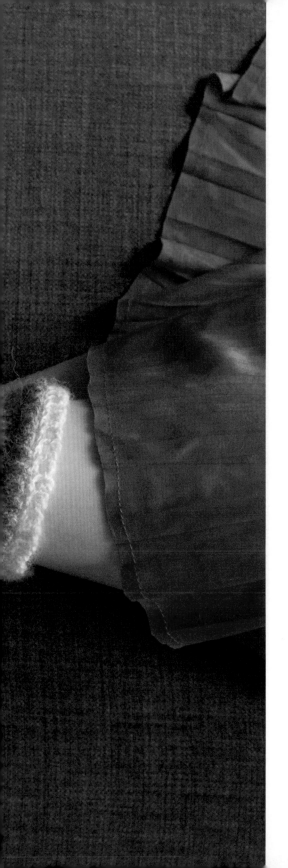

Sizes: 1 (2)
To fit foot circumference: 20 (23) cm / 8 (9)"
– to be worn with approximately 2.5 cm / 1"
negative ease
Finished leg length: 15 (16.5) cm / 6 (6½)"

Yarn: A: Toft Alpaca Fine Sock (4ply/Fingering
weight; 80% British alpaca, 20% nylon; 230 m /
252 yds per 50 g skein)
Shade: Steel; 2 (2) skeins
B: Toft Alpaca Silk Extra Fine (4ply/Fingering
weight; 80% British alpaca, 20% silk; 230 m /
252 yds per 50 g skein)
Shade: Cream; 1 (1) skein

Gauge: 36 sts & 42 rows = 10 cm / 4" over
reverse stocking stitch on 2 mm needles after
blocking

Needles: 2 mm / US 0 DPNs **or** circular needle,
80 cm / 32" length for magic loop
Always use a needle size that will result in the
correct gauge after blocking.

Notions: Stitch marker, smooth contrasting
waste yarn in a similar weight, T-pins (optional),
tapestry needle

Notes: These socks are worked from the toe
up with an afterthought heel. An afterthought
heel is easy to replace if it eventually requires
darning. Fine wool and nylon thread can be held
double during the toes and heels for durability
if desired.

PATTERN BEGINS (make 2 alike)
TOE
Using yarn B and the Turkish method, cast on 32 (36) sts – 16 (18) sts on each needle.
Knit 1 round, and if working with DPNs, divide the stitches evenly across the four needles. Join for working in the round being careful not to twist. PM to indicate beg of round.
Round 1: [K1, M1R, k14 (16), M1L, k1] twice. *36 (40) sts*
Round 2: Knit.
Round 3: [K1, M1R, k16 (18), M1L, k1] twice. *40 (44) sts*
Round 4: Knit.
Continue as set increasing 4 sts every other round until there are 64 (72) sts on the needle, ending with a knit round.
Next round: K16 (18) sts, yo, k to end. *65 (73) sts*
Next round: K to yo, k1 tbl, k to end.
Next round: Knit.
Break yarn B, leaving a tail to weave in later.
FOOT
Join yarn A and work textured pattern as follows:
Round 1: K10 (12), [sl1, k2] 5 times, k8 (10), p to end.
Round 2: P10 (12), [k1, p2] 5 times, p8 (10), p to end.
Round 3: P10 (12), [sl1, p2] 5 times, p8 (10), p to end.
Round 4: P10 (12), [k1, p2] 5 times, p8 (10), p to end.
Rounds 5-10: Rep rounds 3 & 4 three times.
Round 11: P13 (15), [sl1, p2] 3 times, p11 (13), p to end
Round 12: P13 (15), [k1, p2] 3 times, p11 (13), p to end.
Rounds 13-18: Rep rounds 11 & 12 three times.
Round 19: P16 (18), sl1, p16 (18), p to end.
Round 20: P16 (18), k1, p16 (18), p to end.
Rounds 21-26: Rep rounds 19 & 20 three times.
Sock should measure approximately 9 cm / 3½" from cast-on.
Purl all rounds until length from cast-on is 6 cm / 2½" shorter than desired length of foot.

Next round (place afterthought heel marker):
P33 (37) sts, using waste yarn p32 (36) sts to end of round. Slip sts back to working needle and using yarn A purl across waste yarn sts to end of round.
LEG
Continue to purl every round until leg measures 4 (5) cm / 1½ (2)" from waste yarn.
Work textured pattern as follows:
Round 1: P16 (18), sl1, p16 (18), p to end.
Round 2: P16 (18), k1, p16 (18), p to end.
Rounds 3-8: Rep rounds 1 & 2 three times.
Round 9: P13 (15), [sl1, p2] 3 times, p11 (13), p to end.
Round 10: P13 (15), [k1, p2] 3 times, p11 (13), p to end.
Rounds 11-16: Rep rounds 9 & 10 three times.
Round 11: P10 (12), [sl1, p2] 5 times, p8 (10), p to end.
Round 12: P10 (12), [k1, p2] 5 times, p8 (10), p to end.
Rounds 13-18: Rep rounds 11 & 12 three times.
Round 19: P7 (9), [sl1, p2] 7 times, p5 (7), p to end.
Round 20: P7 (9), [k1, p2] 7 times, p5 (7), p to end.
Rounds 21-26: Rep rounds 19 & 20 three times.
Round 27: P4 (6), [sl1, p2] 9 times, p2 (4), p to end.
Round 28: P4 (6), [k1, p2] 9 times, p2 (4), p to end.
Rounds 29-34: Rep rounds 27 & 28 three times.
Round 35: P1 (3), [sl1, p2] 10 times, sl1, p1 (3), p to end.
Round 36: P1 (3), [k1, p2] 10 times, sl1, p1 (3), p to end.
Rounds 37 & 38: Rep rounds 35 & 36 three times.
Round 39: P2tog, p to end of round. *64 (72) sts*
PICOT CUFF
Knit 5 rounds.
Next round: [Yo, k2tog] to end.
Knit 5 rounds.
Break yarn A leaving a long tail to sew down picot hem (approximately three times the circumference of your sock).

Turn sock inside out and thread tapestry needle with yarn B. Starting at the beginning of the round and working clockwise, slip the stitches on to yarn B, remove DPNs and tapestry needle (the threaded yarn B will be used to help work the lace trim later).

Fold down the hem so that you are pleased with the way your picots look and make a note of where the edge lands – this is the purl row you will be sewing into.

Using the long tail of yarn A and a tapestry needle, leaving threaded yarn B in place throughout, sew purlwise through the first live stitch of the round. Next, going from top to bottom with the tapestry needle sew through the corresponding purl bump of the previously noted row.

Continue working like this, working purlwise through next stitch, then top to bottom through next purl bump on the corresponding stitch below it.

Once all stitches are sewn down, weave in yarn A tail.

HEEL

Using working needle, pick up (without knitting) 32 (36) sts along the bottom of the waste yarn, then pick up (without knitting) 32 (36) sts along the top of the waste yarn. Carefully remove the waste yarn. *64 (72) sts*

Pick up 1 st from gap between top and bottom heel sts. Knit this st through the back loop to twist it, k32 (36) sts, pick up 1 st from opposite gap, and knit this st through the back loop to twist it. Repeat this step across the top (or other half) of the heel. *68 (76) sts*

Knit 2 rounds.

Shape the heel as follows:
Round 1: [K1, ssk, k to 3 before end of this half, k2tog, k1] twice. *4 sts dec*
Round 2: Knit.
Rep these rounds 1 & 2 until 32 (36) sts remain, ending with a knit round.

Graft the sts together using Kitchener Stitch.

LACE TRIM

Give the cuff a stretch and you'll see yarn B still threaded around the sock. With working needle and working end of yarn B, pick up and k64 (72) sts anti-clockwise by knitting into the yarn B in-between where you sewed the picot edging down.

Using the backwards loop method, cast 4 sts onto RH needle. Turn work.

Set-up row: K3, ssk (working last st of RH needle and 1 st of LH needle together), turn.
Row 1: Sl1 wyif, k2, [yo] twice, k1, turn.
Row 2: K2, p2, k1, ssk.
Row 3: Sl1 wyif, k5, turn.
Row 4: Cast off 2 sts, k2, ssk.
Rep rows 1-4 until 1 st remains from cuff.
Work rows 1-3 only once more.
Cast off remaining 6 sts.
Break yarn leaving a tail to sew the two lace edges together, then weave in tail.

FINISHING

Weave in ends. Block to measurements and lay flat to dry using T-pins to stretch out the lace out if desired.

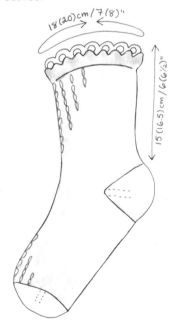

Sizes: 1 (2)

To fit head circumference up to: 51 (56) cm / 20 (22)" – to be worn with 7.5-10 cm / 3-4" negative ease

Finished circumference: 40.5 (46) cm / 16 (18)" circumference

Finished height: 23 (24) cm / 9 (9½)" with brim folded up

Yarn: Handmaiden Fine Yarn Lady Godiva (DK weight; 50% wool, 50% silk; 250 m / 273 yds per 100 g skein)
Shade: Plum; 1 (1) skein

Note: You will need 2 skeins to make the Hat and matching Mitts

Gauge: 26 sts & 28 rows = 10 cm / 4" over Twisted Rib on 3.75 mm needles after blocking

Needles: 3.25 mm / US 3 circular needle, 40 cm / 16" length
3.75 mm / US 5 circular needle, 40 cm / 16" length
3.75 mm / US 5 DPNs for crown shaping
Always use a needle size that will result in the correct gauge after blocking.

Notions: 2 stitch markers, tapestry needle

CABLES

1/1 LT: Slip 1 st to cable needle and hold at front, k1 tbl, then k1 tbl from cable needle.

1/1 RT: Slip 1 st to cable needle and hold at back, k1 tbl, then k1 tbl from cable needle.

1/1 LFT: Slip 1 st to cable needle and hold at front, k1, then k1 tbl from cable needle.

1/1 RFT: Slip 1 st to cable needle and hold at back, k1 tbl, then k1 from cable needle.

1/1 LPT: Slip 1 st to cable needle and hold at front, p1, then k1 tbl from cable needle.

1/1 RPT: Slip 1 st to cable needle and hold at back, k1 tbl, then p1 from cable needle.

ARROW PANEL – WRITTEN INSTRUCTIONS
(worked over 61 sts and 32 rows)

Row 1: [P3, 1/1 RFT, k1 tbl, p1, k1 tbl, 1/1 LFT, p2] 5 times, p1.

Row 2: [P3, k1 tbl, k1, k1 tbl, p1, k1 tbl, k1, k1 tbl, p2] 5 times, p1.

Row 3: [P2, 1/1 RFT, k1, k1 tbl, p1, k1 tbl, k1, 1/1 LFT, p1] 5 times, p1.

Row 4: [P2, k1 tbl, k2, k1 tbl, p1, k1 tbl, k2, k1 tbl, p1] 5 times, p1.

Row 5: [P1, 1/1 RFT, k2, k1 tbl, p1, k1 tbl, k2, 1/1 LFT] 5 times, p1.

Row 6: [P1, k1 tbl, k3, k1 tbl, p1, k1 tbl, k3, k1 tbl] 5 times, p1.

Row 7: [P1, k1 tbl, k2, 1/1 RPT, p1, 1/1 LPT, k2, k1 tbl] 5 times, p1.

Row 8: [P1, k1 tbl, k2, k1 tbl, p3, k1 tbl, k2, k1 tbl] 5 times, p1.

Row 9: [P1, k1 tbl, k1, 1/1 RPT, p3, 1/1 LPT, k1, k1 tbl] 5 times, p1.

Row 10: [P1, k1 tbl, k1, k1 tbl, p5, k1 tbl, k1, k1 tbl] 5 times, p1.

Row 11: [P1, k1 tbl, 1/1 RPT, p5, 1/1 LPT, k1 tbl] 5 times, p1.

Row 12: P1, k2 tbl, p7, k2 tbl, [p1, k2 tbl, p2, k1 tbl, p1, k1 tbl, p2, k2 tbl] 3 times, p1, k2 tbl, p7, k2 tbl, p1.

Row 13: P1, 1/1 RPT, p1, p2tog, p1 ssp, p1, 1/1 LPT, [p1, 1/1 RPT, p1, 1/1 RT, p1, 1/1 LT, p1, 1/1 LPT] 3 times, p1, 1/1 RPT, p1, p2tog, p1, ssp, p1, 1/1 LPT, p1.

Row 14: P10, [p4, k2 tbl, p1, k2 tbl, p3] 3 times, p11.

Row 15: P10, [p3, 1/1 RFT, k1 tbl, p1, k1 tbl, 1/1 LFT, p2] 3 times, p11.

Row 16: P10, [p3, k1 tbl, k1, k1 tbl, p1, k1 tbl, k1, k1 tbl, p2] 3 times, p11.

Row 17: P10, [p2, 1/1 RFT, k1, k1 tbl, p1, k1 tbl, k1, 1/1 LFT, p1] 3 times, p11.

Row 18: P10, [p2, k1 tbl, k2, k1 tbl, p1, k1 tbl, k2, k1 tbl, p1] 3 times, p11.

Row 19: P10, [p1, 1/1 RFT, k2, k1 tbl, p1, k1 tbl, k2, 1/1 LFT] 3 times, p11.

Row 20: P10, [p1, k1 tbl, k3, k1 tbl, p1, k1 tbl, k3, k1 tbl] 3 times, p11.

Row 21: P10, [p1, k1 tbl, k2, 1/1 RPT, p1, 1/1 LPT, k2, k1 tbl] 3 times, p11.

Row 22: P10, [p1, k1 tbl, k2, k1 tbl, p3, k1 tbl, k2, k1 tbl] 3 times, p11.

Row 23: P10, [p1, k1 tbl, k1, 1/1 RPT, p3, 1/1 LPT, k1, k1 tbl] 3 times, p11.

Row 24: P10, [p1, k1 tbl, k1, k1 tbl, p5, k1 tbl, k1, k1 tbl] 3 times, p11.

Row 25: P10, [p1, k1 tbl, 1/1 RPT, p5, 1/1 LPT, k1 tbl] 3 times, p11.

Row 26: P11, k2 tbl, p7, k2 tbl, p1, k2 tbl, p2, k1 tbl, p1, k1 tbl, p2, k2 tbl, p1, k2 tbl, p7, k2 tbl, p11.

Row 27: P11, 1/1 RPT, p1, p2tog, p1, ssp, p1, 1/1

LPT, p1, 1/1 RPT, p1, 1/1 RT, p1, 1/1 LT, p1, 1/1 LPT, p1, 1/1 RPT, p1, p2tog, p1, ssp, p1, 1/1 LPT, p11.

Row 28: P24, k2 tbl, p1, k2 tbl, p24.

Row 29: P23, 1/1 RFT, k1 tbl, p1, k1 tbl, 1/1 LFT, p23.

Row 30: P23, k1 tbl, k1, k1 tbl, p1, k1 tbl, k1, k1 tbl, p23.

Row 31: P22, 1/1 RFT, k1, k1 tbl, p1, k1 tbl, k1, 1/1 LFT, p22.

Row 32: P22, k1 tbl, k2, k1 tbl, p1, k1 tbl, k2, k1 tbl, p22.

PATTERN BEGINS
BRIM

Using smaller needles and the long-tail method, cast on 116 (122) sts.

Set-up round: [P1 tbl, k1 tbl] to end, do not turn and join for working in the round being careful not to twist. PM to indicate beg of round.
This sets Twisted Rib.
Work Twisted Rib until hat measures 7.5 (9) cm / 3 (3½)" from cast-on edge.

Change to larger needles and work Twisted Rib for a further 5 rounds.

Next round: Work Twisted Rib across 61 sts, PM, work Twisted Rib to end.

SET-UP FOR MAIN BODY

Rounds 1 & 2: [P1, k1 tbl, p3, k1 tbl, p1, k1 tbl, p3, k1 tbl] 5 times, p1, SM, p1, [p1, k1 tbl] to last 2 sts, p2.

Round 3: [P1, k1 tbl, p2, 1/1 RT, p1, 1/1 LT, p2, k1 tbl] 5 times, p1, SM, p1, [p1, k1 tbl] to last 2 sts, p2.

Round 4: [P1, k1 tbl, p2, k2 tbl, p1, k2 tbl, p2, k1 tbl] 5 times, p1, SM, p1, [p1, k1 tbl] to last 2 sts, p2.

MAIN BODY

Round 1: Reading from the Chart or Written Instructions, work row 1 of Arrow Panel (p 81) to marker, SM, p2tog, p2, [k1 tbl, p1] to last 3 sts, p1, ssp. *114 (120) sts*

Rounds 2-4: Work next row of Arrow Panel to marker, SM, p3, [k1 tbl, p1] to last 2 sts, p2.

Note: Arrow Panel is now referred to as 'patt'. Work the next row of panel with each consecutive round.

Round 5: Patt to marker, SM, p2tog, p3, [k1 tbl, p1] to last 4 sts, p2, ssp. *112 (118) sts*

Rounds 6-8: Patt to marker, SM, p4, [k1 tbl, p1] to last 3 sts, p3.

Round 9: Patt to marker, SM, p2tog, p4, [k1 tbl, p1] to last 5 sts, p3, ssp. *110 (116) sts*

Rounds 10-12: Patt to marker, SM, p5, [k1 tbl, p1] to last 4 sts, p4.

Round 13: Patt to marker, SM, p2tog, p5, [k1 tbl, p1] to last 6 sts, p4, ssp. *104 (110) sts*

Rounds 14-16: Patt to marker, SM, p6, [k1 tbl, p1] last 5 sts, p5.

Round 17: Patt to marker, SM, p2tog, p6, [k1 tbl, p1] to last 7 sts, p5, ssp. *102 (108) sts*

Rounds 18-20: Patt to marker, SM, p7, [k1 tbl, p1] to last 6 sts, p6.

Round 21: Patt to marker, SM, p2tog, p7, [k1 tbl, p1] to last 8 sts, p6, ssp. *100 (106) sts*

Rounds 22-24: Patt to marker, SM, p8, [k1 tbl, p1] to last 7 sts, p7.

Round 25: Patt to marker, SM, p2tog, p8, [k1 tbl, p1] to last 9 sts, p7, ssp. *98 (104) sts*

Round 26: Patt to marker, SM, p9, [k1 tbl, p1] to last 8 sts, p8.

Round 27: Patt to marker, SM, p9, [k1 tbl, p1] to last 8 sts, p8. *94 (100) sts*

Round 28: Patt to marker, SM, p9, [k1 tbl, p1] to last 8 sts, p8.

Round 29: Patt to marker, SM, p2tog, p9, [k1 tbl, p1] to last 10 sts, p8, ssp. *92 (98) sts*

Rounds 30-32: Patt to marker, SM, p10, [k1 tbl, p1] to last 9 sts, p9.

CROWN

Continue as follows to shape the crown, switching to DPNs as required:

Round 1: [P2, p2tog] 5 times, p1, 1/1 RFT, k2, k1 tbl, p1, k1 tbl, k2, 1/1 LFT, p1, [p2, p2tog] 7 times, p4, [k1 tbl, p1] 8 (11) times, p3, [p2, p2tog] twice. *78 (84) sts*

Round 2: P16, k1 tbl, k3, k1 tbl, p1, k1 tbl, k3, k1 tbl, p26, [k1 tbl, p1] 8 (11) times, p9.

Round 3: P16, k1 tbl, k2, 1/1 RPT, p1, 1/1 LPT, k2, k1 tbl, p26, [k1 tbl, p1] 8 (11) times, p9.

Round 4: P16, k1 tbl, k2, k1 tbl, p1, k1 tbl, k2, k1 tbl, p26, [k1 tbl, p1] 8 (11) times, p9.

Round 5: [P1, p2tog] 5 times, p1, k1 tbl, k1, 1/1 RPT, p3, 1/1 LPT, k1, k1 tbl, p1, [p1, p2tog] 8 times, p3, [k1 tbl, p1] 6 (9) times, p2, [p1, p2tog] 3 times. *62 (68) sts*

Round 6: P11, k1 tbl, k1, k1 tbl, p5, k1 tbl, k1, k1 tbl, p20, [k1 tbl, p1] 6 (9) times, p8.

Round 7: P11, k1 tbl, 1/1 RPT, p5, 1/1 LPT, k1 tbl, p20, [k1 tbl, p1] 6 (9) times, p8.

Round 8: P11, k2 tbl, p7, k2 tbl, p20, [k1 tbl, p1] 6 (9) times, p8.

Round 9: [P2tog] 5 times, p1, 1/1 RPT, p1, p2tog, p1, ssp, p1, 1/1 LPT, p1, [p2tog] 9 times, p3, [k1 tbl, p1] 4 (7) times, p2, [p2tog] 4 times. *42 (48) sts*

Round 10: P6, k1 tbl, p7, k1 tbl, p13, [k1 tbl, p1] 4 (7) times, p6.

Round 11: [P2tog] 3 times, k1 tbl, p1, p2tog, p1, ssp, p1, k1 tbl, [p2tog] 6 times, p1, [k1 tbl, p1] 4 (7) times, [p2tog] 3 times. *28 (34) sts*

Round 12: P1, p2tog, k1 tbl, p2tog, p1, ssp, k1 tbl, [p1, p2tog] twice, p1, [ssk] 4 (7) times, p1, p2tog. *18 (21) sts*
Break yarn and thread tail through remaining sts.

FINISHING

Weave in ends and gently block to measurements laying the hat flat to dry and taking care not to overstretch the rib.

23 (24) cm / 9 (9½)"

40.5 (46) cm / 16 (18)"

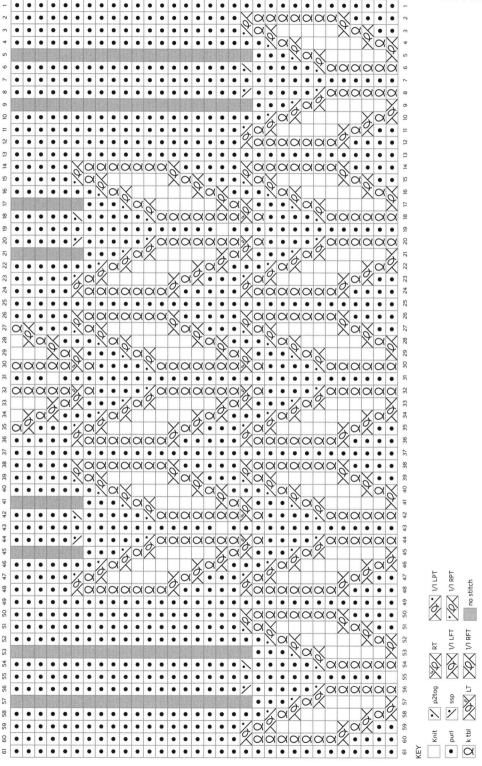

CASWELL BAY

KEY

Knit	
•	purl
ℚ	k tbl

p2tog	ssp	LT	
RT	1/1 LFT	1/1 RFT	
1/1 LPT	1/1 RPT	no stitch	

Sizes: 1 (2)

To fit hand circumference up to: 20 (23) cm / 8 (9)" – to be worn with up to 7 (8) cm / 2¾ (3¼)" negative ease

Finished circumference: 13 (15) cm / 5 (6)" circumference

Finished length: 22 cm / 8½" length

Yarn: Handmaiden Fine Yarn Lady Godiva (DK weight; 50% wool, 50% silk; 250 m / 273 yds per 100 g skein)

Shade: Plum; 1 (1) skein

Note: You will need 2 skeins to make the Mitts and matching Hat

Gauge: 32 sts & 34 rows = 10 cm / 4" over Twisted Rib (unstretched) on 3.25 mm needles after blocking

15 sts & 18 rows = 5 cm / 2" over Arrow Panel on 3.25 mm needles after blocking

Needles: 3.25 mm / US 3 DPNs **or** circular needle, 80 cm / 32" length for magic loop Always use a needle size that will result in the correct gauge after blocking.

Notions: 5 stitch markers, cable needle, stitch holder or waste yarn, tapestry needle.

Notes: Whilst the mitts use the same stitch pattern as the Caswell Bay Hat, the gauge is tighter to produce a denser fabric more suited to warm mitts.

Stitch Glossary

CABLES

1/1 LT: Slip 1 st to cable needle and hold at front, k1 tbl, then k1 tbl from cable needle.

1/1 RT: Slip 1 st to cable needle and hold at back, k1 tbl, then k1 tbl from cable needle.

1/1 LFT: Slip 1 st to cable needle and hold at front, k1, then k1 tbl from cable needle.

1/1 RFT: Slip 1 st to cable needle and hold at back, k1 tbl, then k1 from cable needle.

1/1 LPT: Slip 1 st to cable needle and hold at front, p1, then k1 tbl from cable needle.

1/1 RPT: Slip 1 st to cable needle and hold at back, k1 tbl, then p1 from cable needle.

TWISTED 1x1 RIB

[K1 tbl, p1] every round.

ARROW PANEL – WRITTEN INSTRUCTIONS (worked over 15 sts)

Rows 1-8: P2, [k1 tbl, p1] 5 times, k1 tbl, p2.

Rows 9-10: P2, k1 tbl, p3, k1 tbl, p1, k1 tbl, p3, k1 tbl, p2.

Row 11: P2, k1 tbl, p2, 1/1 RT, p1, 1/1 LT, p2, k1 tbl, p2.

Row 12: P2, k1 tbl, p2, k2 tbl, p1, k2 tbl, p2, k1 tbl, p2.

Row 13: P4, 1/1 RFT, k1 tbl, p1, k1 tbl, 1/1 LFT, p4.

Row 14: P4, k1 tbl, k1, k1 tbl, p1, k1 tbl, k1, k1 tbl, p4.

Row 15: P3, 1/1 RFT, k1, k1 tbl, p1, k1 tbl, k1, 1/1 LFT, p3.

Row 16: P3, k1 tbl, k2, k1 tbl, p1, k1 tbl, k2, k1 tbl, p3.

Row 17: P2, 1/1 RFT, k2, k1 tbl, p1, k1 tbl, k2, 1/1 LFT, p2.

Row 18: P2, k1 tbl, k3, k1 tbl, p1, k1 tbl, k3, k1 tbl, p2.

Row 19: P2, k1 tbl, k2, 1/1 RPT, p1, 1/1 LPT, k2, k1 tbl, p2.

Row 20: P2, k1 tbl, k2, k1 tbl, p3, k1 tbl, k2, k1 tbl, p2.

Row 21: P2, k1 tbl, k1, 1/1 RPT, p3, 1/1 LPT, k1, k1 tbl, p2.

Row 22: P2, k1 tbl, k1, k1 tbl, p5, k1 tbl, k1, k1 tbl, p2.

Row 23: P2, k1 tbl, 1/1 RPT, p5, 1/1 LPT, k1 tbl, p2.

Row 24: P2, k2 tbl, p2, k1 tbl, p1, k1 tbl, p2, k2 tbl, p2.

Row 25: P2, 1/1 RPT, p1, 1/1 RT, p1, 1/1 LT, p1, 1/1 LPT, p2.

Row 26: P5, k2 tbl, p1, k2 tbl, p5.

Rows 27-38: As rows 13-24.

Row 39: P2, 1/1 RPT, p2, k1 tbl, p1, k1 tbl, p2, 1/1 LPT, p2.

Rows 40-41: As rows 9-10.

Rows 42-47: As rows 1-6.

PATTERN BEGINS

Using the long-tail method, cast on 40 (44) sts. Join for working in the round being careful not to twist. PM to indicate beg of round.

CUFF

Round 1: K1 tbl, PM, reading from the Chart or Written Instructions work row 1 of Arrow Panel across next 15 sts, PM, [k1 tbl, p1] to end.

Round 2: K1 tbl, SM, work row 2 of Arrow Panel across next 15 sts, SM, [k1 tbl, p1] to end.

Continue as set in Twisted Rib pattern, working the next row of Arrow Panel with each round, to end of row 26 of Arrow Panel.

Rep Rounds 13-26 once more.

GUSSET

Continuing to work one more rep of rounds 13-26 as set, commence thumb gusset working the Right and Left mitt set-up differently as follows:

Right Mitt Gusset Set-Up

Round 1: Patt 18 (20) sts, PM, M1R, k1 tbl, p1, k1 tbl, M1L, PM, patt to end. *2 sts inc; 5 sts between gusset markers*

Left Mitt Gusset Set Up

Round 1: Patt 36 (38) sts, PM, M1R, k1 tbl, p1, k1 tbl, M1L, PM, patt to end. *2 sts inc; 5 sts between gusset markers*

BOTH Mitts

Continue working Twisted Rib and Arrow Panel as set and work gusset between markers as follows, increasing every other round as instructed:

Round 2: K2 tbl, p1, k2 tbl.

Round 3: K1 tbl, M1P, k1 tbl, p1, k1 tbl, M1P, k1 tbl. *7 sts*

Round 4: [K1 tbl, p1] 3 times, k1 tbl.

Round 5: K1 tbl, p1, M1R, k1 tbl, p1, k1 tbl, M1L, p1, k1 tbl. *9 sts*

Round 6: K1 tbl, p1, k2 tbl, p1, k2 tbl, p1, k1 tbl.

Round 7: K1 tbl, p1, k1 tbl, M1P, k1 tbl, p1, k1 tbl, M1P, k1 tbl, p1, k1 tbl. *11 sts*

Round 8: [K1 tbl, p1] 5 times, k1 tbl.

Round 9: [K1 tbl, p1] twice, M1R, k1 tbl, p1, k1 tbl, M1L, [p1, k1 tbl] twice. *13 sts*

Round 10: [K1 tbl, p1] twice, k2 tbl, p1, k2 tbl, [p1, k1 tbl] twice.

Round 11: [K1 tbl, p1] twice, k1 tbl, M1P, k1 tbl, p1, k1 tbl, M1P, k1 tbl, [p1, k1 tbl] twice. *15 (15) sts between gusset markers; 52 (56) sts total*

Rounds 12-14: [K1 tbl, p1] 7 times, k1 tbl.

Round 15: K1 tbl, SM, work row 27 of Arrow Panel, SM, patt to gusset marker, remove gusset markers and place next 15 sts on stitch holder or waste yarn, cast on 3 sts to close gap, patt to end of round. *40 (44) sts total*

HAND

Work straight in Twisted Rib and Arrow Panel as set working through rows 28-47 of Arrow Panel once. Work reps of last round if you want to add extra length to the top of the mitt. Cast off in rib pattern.

Repeat instructions for second mitt taking care to place the gusset correctly.

THUMB (both sizes alike)

Place the 15 held thumb sts on working needles.

Round 1: Work Twisted Rib as set across the next 15 sts, pick up and work 3 sts across the gap in Twisted Rib. Join for working in the round and PM to indicate beg of round. *18 sts*

Work Twisted Rib for 5 rounds.

If you would like extra length in the thumb, continue in Twisted Rib for another few rounds.

Cast off in Twisted Rib.

FINISHING

Weave in ends and block gently, laying flat to dry.

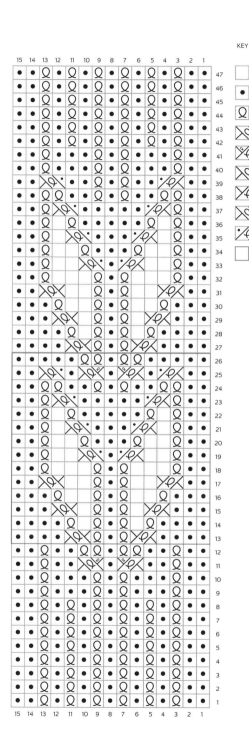

KEY

- ☐ knit
- • purl
- Ϙ k tbl
- ⤬ 1/1 LT
- ⤬ 1/1 RT
- ⤬ 1/1 LFT
- ⤬ 1/1 RFT
- ⤬ 1/1 LPT
- ⤬ 1/1 RPT
- ☐ Repeat

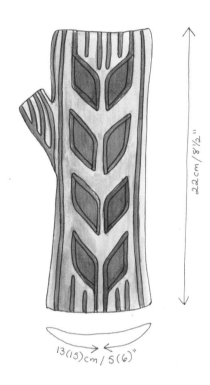

22cm / 8½"

13(15)cm / 5(6)"

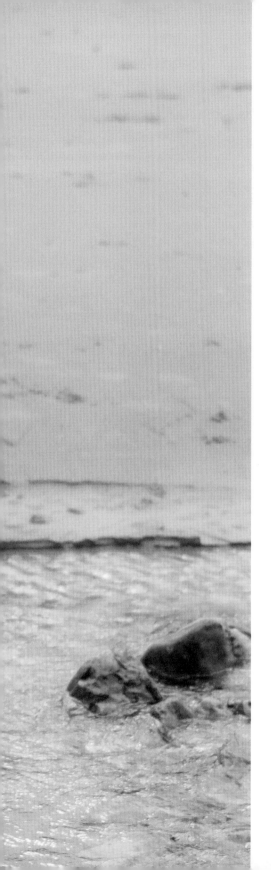

Sizes: 1 (2, 3)

To fit head circumference: 51 (53, 56) cm / 20 (21, 22)" – to be worn with approximately 5 cm / 2" negative ease

Finished circumference: 46 (48, 51) cm / 18 (19, 20)"

Width: 9 cm / 3½" wide

Yarn: **Illimani** Silky Baby Llama (worsted weight; 70% Baby Llama, 30% Mulberry Silk; 200 m / 220 yds per 100 g skein)
Shade: Ginger; 1 (1, 1) skein

Gauge: 41 sts x 22 rows = 9 cm / 3½" over cable pattern after blocking

Needles: 4.5 mm / US 4 knitting needles
4.5 mm / US 7 **or** 5 mm / US H/8 crochet hook for provisional cast-on
Always use a needle size that will result in the correct gauge after blocking.

Notions: Smooth waste yarn in a similar weight for provisional cast-on, cable needle, tapestry needle

CABLES

4/4 LPC: Slip 4 sts to cable needle and hold at front, k2, p2 from needle, k2, p2 from cable needle.

4/4 RPC: Slip 4 sts to cable needle and hold at back, p2, k2 from needle, p2, k2 from cable needle.

CHART – WRITTEN INSTRUCTIONS
(worked over 41 sts and 8 rows)

Row 1 (RS): [P2, k2] 3 times, 4/4 RPC, p1, 4/4 LPC, [k2, p2] 3 times.

Row 2 (WS and all following WS rows): [K2, p2] 5 times, k1, [p2, k2] 5 times.

Row 3: [P2, k2] twice, 4/4 RPC, p2, k2, p1, k2, p2, 4/4 LPC, [k2, p2] twice.

Row 5: P2, k2, 4/4 RPC, [p2, k2] twice, p1, [k2, p2] twice, 4/4 LPC, k2, p2.

Row 7: 4/4 RPC, [p2, k2] 3 times, p1, [k2, p2] 3 times, 4/4 LPC.

PATTERN BEGINS

Using the provisional crochet method, cast on 41 sts.

Set-up row (WS): Using the main yarn, [k2, p2] 5 times, k1, [p2, k2] 5 times.

Reading from the Chart or Written Instructions, work the 8-row repeat a total of 13 (14, 15) times then repeat rows 1-7 only once more.

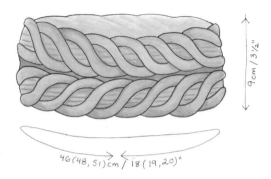

46 (48, 51) cm / 18 (19, 20)"

Do not cast off! Break yarn leaving a long tail for grafting.

Unzip the provisional cast-on, and graft the two ends together using Kitchener Stitch in 2x2 ribbing.

Note: Owing to the rib pattern, it will be tricky to unravel the provisional cast-on smoothly. We suggest picking up the stitches which are sitting on the waste yarn (using a smaller needle if necessary) and very carefully snip the waste yarn to release the stitches.

FINISHING

Weave in ends and very gently block, laying the headband flat to dry and taking care not to overstretch the fabric.

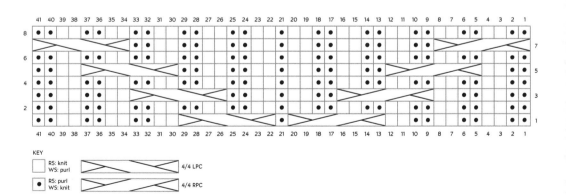

One size: 208 cm / 82" wide x 33 cm / 13" deep at deepest point and 8 cm / 3¼" deep at narrowest point

Yarn: **Kettle Yarn Co.** Islington DK (55% Blue Faced Leicester wool, 45% silk, 212 m / 232 yds per 100 g skein)
Shade: Icicle; 3 skeins

Gauge: 16 sts & 22 rows = 10 cm / 4" over pattern on 4.5 mm needles after blocking

Needles: 4.5 mm / US 7 circular needle, 100 cm / 40" length **AND** additional spare 4.5 mm / US 7 of similar or shorter length
Always use a needle size that will result in the correct gauge after blocking.

Notions: 4 stitch markers, tapestry needle

Notes: The border is worked in 3 separate pieces and then joined together before working in short rows to create the shape. The shawl is finished with an i-cord cast off.

PATTERN BEGINS
SET-UP
Left Border (LB)
Using the spare circular needle and long-tail method, cast on 124 sts.
Row 1 (WS): P3, [k2, p2] to last st, p1.
Row 2 (RS): K3, [p2, k2] to last st, k1.
Rep rows 1 and 2 twice more then row 1 only again.
Break yarn, leaving a tail to weave in later. With RS facing slip Left Border sts to main circular needle.

Centre Border (CB)
Using the spare circular needle and long-tail method, cast on 64 sts.
Row 1: (WS): P3, [k2, p2] to last st, p1.
Row 2: (RS): K3, [p2, k2] to last st, k1.
Rep rows 1 and 2 twice more then row 1 only again.
Break yarn, leaving a tail to weave in later. With RS facing slip Centre Border sts to main circular needle.

Right Border (RB)
Work as for Left Border but do not break yarn at the end. With RS facing slip Right Border sts to main needle.
The Left, Centre and Right Borders should be lined up on the main needle with RS facing. *312 sts on the needle*

Join the three border sections as follows:
Set-up row 1 (RS): K119, PM, p2, k3, using the backwards loop method, cast on 15 sts, working across CB, k19, PM, p2, k22, p2, PM, k19, using the backwards loop method, cast on 15 sts, working across LB, k3, p2, PM, k16, w&t. *342 sts*
Set-up row 2 (WS): [K1, p1] to marker, SM, k2, p to marker, SM, k2, [k1, p1] to 2 sts before marker, k2, SM, p to 2 sts before marker, k2, SM, [k1, p1] across next 16 sts, w&t.

MAIN SHAWL BODY – SECTION 1
Short row 1 (RS): K to marker, SM, p2, k2, yo, sssk, [yo, ssk] to 2 sts before marker, yo, k2, SM, p2, k22, p2, SM, k2, [yo, k2tog] to 7 sts before marker, yo, k3tog, yo, k2, p2, SM, k to 2 sts past wrapped st (working the wrap with the stitch as you pass it), w&t.
Short row 2 (WS): [K1, p1] to 1 st before marker, k1, SM, k2, p to marker, SM, k2, [p1, k1] to 2 sts before marker, k2, SM, p to 2 sts before marker, k2, SM, [p1, k1] to 2 sts past wrapped st (working the wrap with the stitch as you pass it), w&t.

Continue working in short rows as follows and as you come to a wrapped stitch, pick up the wrap and knit or purl together with the stitch it wraps:
Short row 3: K to marker, SM, p2, k2, yo, sssk, [yo, ssk], to 2 sts before marker, yo, k2, SM, p2, k22, p2, SM, k2, [yo, k2tog] to 7 sts before marker, yo, k3tog, yo, k2, p2, SM, k to 2 sts past wrapped st, w&t.
Short row 4: [K1, p1] to marker, SM, k2, p to marker, SM, k2, [k1, p1] to 2 sts before marker, k2, SM, p to 2 sts before marker, k2, SM, [k1, p1] to 2 sts past wrapped st, w&t.
Short rows 5-12: Rep last 4 short rows twice more.
Short row 13: K to marker, M1L, SM, p2, k1, ssk, [ssk, yo] to 2 sts before marker, k2, SM, p2, k22, p2, SM, k2, [yo, k2tog] to 5 sts before marker, k2tog, k1, p2, SM, M1R, k to 2 sts past wrapped st, w&t.
Short row 14: [K1, p1] to marker, SM, k2, p to marker, SM, k2, [p1, k1] to 2 sts before marker, k2, SM, p to 2 sts before marker, k2, SM, [k1, p1] to 2 sts past wrapped st, w&t.
Short row 15: K to marker, M1L, SM, p2, k1, sssk, [yo, ssk] to 2 sts before marker, yo, k2, SM, p2, k22, p2, SM, k2, [yo, k2tog] to 6 sts before marker, yo, k3tog, k1, p2, SM, M1R, k to 2 sts past wrapped st, w&t.
Short row 16: [K1, p1] to marker, SM, k2, p to marker, SM, k2, [k1, p1] to 2 sts before marker, k2, SM, p to 2 sts before marker, k2, SM, [k1, p1] to 2 sts past wrapped st, w&t.
Short rows 17-20: Rep last 4 short rows once more.

Short row 21: K to marker, M1L, SM, p2, k1, ssk, [ssk, yo] to last 4 sts before marker, k3tog, k1, SM, p2, M1R, k to last 2 sts before marker, M1L, p2, SM, k1, sssk, [yo, k2tog] to last 5 sts before marker, k2tog, k1, p2, SM, M1R, k to 2 sts past wrapped st, w&t. *340 sts*

Short row 22: [K1, p1] to marker, SM, k2, p to marker, SM, k2, [k1, p1] to 2 sts before marker, k2, SM, p to 2 sts before marker, k2, SM, [k1, p1] to 2 sts past wrapped st, w&t.

Short row 23: K to marker, M1L, SM, p2, k1, sssk, [yo, ssk] to 4 sts before marker, yo, k3tog, k1, SM, p2, M1R, k to 2 sts before marker, M1L, p2, SM, k1, sssk, [yo, k2tog] to 6 sts before marker, yo, k3tog, k1, p2, SM, M1R, k to 2 sts past wrapped st, w&t. *338 sts*

Short row 24: [K1, p1] to marker, SM, k2, p to marker, SM, k2, [k1, p1] to 2 sts before marker, k2, SM, p to 2 sts before marker, k2, SM, [k1, p1] to 2 sts past wrapped st, w&t.

SECTION 2

Short row 1 (RS): K to marker, M1L, SM, p2, k1, ssk, [ssk, yo] to 4 sts before marker, k3tog, k1, SM, p2, M1R, k to 2 sts before marker, M1L, p2, SM, k1, sssk, [yo, k2tog] to last 5 sts before marker, k2tog, k1, p2, SM, M1R, k to 2 sts past wrapped st, w&t. *336 sts*

Short row 2 (WS): [K1, p1] to marker, SM, k2, p to marker, SM, k2, [k1, p1] to 2 sts before marker, k2, SM, p to 2 sts before marker, k2, SM, [k1, p1] to 2 sts past wrapped st, w&t.

Short row 3: K to marker, M1L, SM, p2, k1, sssk, [yo, ssk] to 4 sts before marker, yo, k3tog, k1, SM, p2, M1R, k to 2 sts before marker, M1L, p2, SM, k1, sssk, [yo, k2tog] to 6 sts before marker, yo, k3tog, k1, p2, SM, M1R, k to 2 sts past wrapped st, w&t. *334 sts*

Short row 4: [K1, p1] to marker, SM, k2, p to marker, SM, k2, [k1, p1] to 2 sts before marker, k2, SM, p to 2 sts before marker, k2, SM, [k1, p1] to 2 sts past wrapped st, w&t.

Short rows 5-8: Rep last 4 short rows once more.

SECTION 3

Short row 1 (RS): K to marker, M1L, SM, p2, k1, ssk, [ssk, yo] to 4 sts before marker, k3tog, k1, SM, p2, M1R, kfb, k to 3 sts before marker, kfb, M1L, p2, SM, k1, sssk, [yo, k2tog] to 5 sts before marker, k2tog, k1, p2, SM, M1R, k to 2 sts past wrapped st, w&t.

Short row 2 (WS): [K1, p1] to marker, SM, k2, p to marker, SM, k2, [p1, k1] to 2 sts before marker, k2, SM, p to 2 sts before marker, k2, SM, [k1, p1] to 2 sts past wrapped st, w&t.

Short row 3: K to marker, M1L, SM, p2, k1, sssk, ssk, yo, ssk, k3tog, k1, SM, p2, M1R, kfb, k to 3 sts before marker, kfb, M1L, p2, SM, k1, sssk, k2tog, yo, k2tog, k3tog, k1, p2, SM, M1R, k to 2 sts past wrapped st, w&t. *330 sts*

Short row 4: [K1, p1] to marker, SM, k2, p to marker, SM, k2, [k1, p1] to 2 sts before marker, k2, SM, p to 2 sts before marker, k2, SM, [k1, p1] to 2 sts past wrapped st, w&t.

SECTION 4

Short row 1 (RS): K to marker, M1L, SM, p2, k1, ssk, k3tog, k1, SM, p2, M1R, kfb, k to 3 sts before marker, kfb, M1L, p2, SM, k1, sssk, k2tog, k1, p2, SM, M1R, k to 2 sts past wrapped st, w&t.

Short row 2 (WS): [K1, p1] to marker, SM, k2, p to marker, SM, k2, [p1, k1] to 2 sts before marker, k2, SM, p to 2 sts before marker, k2, SM, [k1, p1] to 2 sts past wrapped st, w&t.

Short row 3: K to marker, SM, p2, k3tog, k1, SM, p2, M1R, kfb, k to 3 sts before marker, kfb, M1L, p2, SM, k1, sssk, p2, SM, k to 2 sts past wrapped st, w&t.

Short row 4: [K1, p1] to 1 st before marker, k1, SM, k2, p2, SM, k2, [k1, p1] to 2 sts before marker, k2, SM, p2, k2, SM, [p1, k1] to 2 sts past wrapped st, w&t.

Short row 5: K to marker, remove marker, k3tog, k1, SM, p2, M1R, kfb, k to 3 sts before marker, kfb, M1L, p2, SM, k1, sssk, remove marker, k to 2 sts past wrapped st, w&t.

Short row 6: [K1, p1] to 2 sts before marker, p2, SM, k2, [p1, k1] to 2 sts before marker, k2, SM, p2, [k1, p1] to 2 sts past wrapped st, w&t.

Short row 7: K to 4 sts before marker, k3tog, k1, SM, p2, M1R, kfb, k to 3 sts before marker, kfb, M1L, p2, SM, k1, sssk, k to 2 sts past wrapped st, w&t.

Short row 8: [K1, p1] to 3 sts before marker, k1, p2, SM, k2, [k1, p1] to 2 sts before marker, k2, SM, p2, [p1, k1] to 2 sts past wrapped st, w&t.

SECTION 5

Short row 1 (RS): K to 4 sts before marker, k3tog, k1, SM, p2, M1R, kfb, k to 3 sts before marker, kfb, M1L, p2, SM, k1, sssk, k to 2 sts past wrapped st, w&t.

Short row 2 (WS): [K1, p1] to 2 sts before marker, p2, SM, k2, [p1, k1] to 2 sts before marker, k2, SM, p2, [k1, p1] to 2 sts past wrapped st, w&t.

Short row 3: K to 4 sts before marker, k3tog, k1, SM, p2, M1R, kfb, k to 3 sts before marker, kfb, M1L, p2, SM, k1, sssk, k to 2 sts past wrapped st, w&t.

Short row 4: [K1, p1] to 3 sts before marker, k1, p2, SM, k2, [k1, p1] to 2 sts before marker, k2, SM, p2, [p1, k1] to 2 sts past wrapped st, w&t. Rep last 4 rows until 3 sts remain unworked on LH needle, ending with row 4.

SECTION 6

Row 1 (RS): Picking up and working the wraps together with the stitch they are wrapping, k to 3 sts before marker, k2tog, k1, SM, p2, M1R, k to 2 sts before marker, M1L, p2, SM, k1, ssk, k to end of row.

Row 2 (WS): Picking up and working the wraps together with the stitch they are wrapping, p3, [k1, p1] to 2 sts before marker, p2, SM, k2, [p1,

k1] to 2 sts before marker, k2, SM, p2, [p1, k1] to last 4 sts, p4. *All wraps are now worked and there are 330 sts on the needle.*

Row 3: K to marker, SM, p2, k to 2 sts before marker, p2, SM, k to end.

Row 4: P4, [k1, p1] to 2 sts before marker, p2, SM, k2, [k1, p1] to 2 sts before marker, k2, SM, p2, [k1, p1] to last 2 sts, p2.

Row 5: K to marker, SM, p2, k to 2 sts before marker, p2, SM, k to end.

Row 6: P3, [p1, k1] to 2 sts before marker, p2, SM, k2, [k1, p1] to 2 sts, k2, SM, p2, [p1, k1] to last 4 sts, p4.

With RS facing, k3, wrap the next st but **do not turn** work. Place 4 sts back on LH needle and work i-cord cast off as follows: *K2, ssk, place the 3 sts back on LH needle; rep from * across the top of the shawl until 3 sts remain unworked on LH needle. Break yarn leaving a long tail and graft the 3 sts on RH needle together with 3 sts on LH needle using Kitchener Stitch.

FINISHING

Weave in ends and block to measurements.

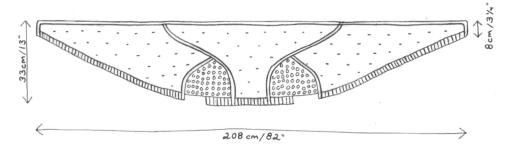

The Uncommon Thread
uncommonthread.co.uk

Kettle Yarn Co.
kettleyarnco.co.uk

SweetGeorgia Yarns
sweetgeorgiayarns.com

John Arbon Textiles
jarbon.com

Illimani Yarn
illimaniyarn.com

TOFT
thetoftalpacashop.co.uk

Handmaiden Fine Yarn
handmaiden.ca

The Border Mill
thebordermill.co.uk

I would like start first by thanking my family and friends back home on the east coast of Canada. This journey would not have been possible without your initial support and belief in my work. There have been many times when you have metaphorically and literally pushed me out the door to pursue my half-formed ideas and dreams. Thank you to my mother, Wendy, for putting knitting needles in my hands and to my father, Vince, for enabling my desire to travel.

There are many inspirational knitters and creative mentors who have influenced my life and work in various ways. Thank you to Anna Whalen, my high school art teacher, for walking me through my first pair of mittens a long time ago. Thank you to Louise King and Eileen Manzuk at LK Yarns in Halifax, for their patience as I learnt how to navigate the stock room and the importance of gauge. Much appreciation goes out to my colleagues at my current yarn shop Loop in London. It's hard not to feel at home when surrounded by yarn and your much-loved company.

It's been an incredible journey with Pom Pom Quarterly to date, I have come to learn a huge amount. Thank you to Meghan, Lydia, and Amy for allowing me to join the team briefly as an intern. It's been a joy to see behind the scenes of your beautiful magazine along with this latest opportunity. This has all been an exciting personal journey. You've been gracious mentors and fast friends.

Many thanks to photographer Juju Vail, for accompanying me and the Pom Pom team to Wales for our photo shoot, and to Lydia's family for being such welcoming hosts during our stay.

There are others who have worked many hours behind the scenes on this project. Thank you to my technical editors Rachel Atkinson and Jemima Bicknell, copy editor Annie Prime, and designer Murray Wyse. Your wealth of talent and knowledge has helped to bring my designs to life on the printed page.

To each yarn company mentioned in this collection, thank you for the yarn support. I hope you continue to provide us knitters with rich colours and delectable fibres for a long time to come.

Thank you to Natalie Selles for being such a great friend and beautiful model. Showing me how to navigate my way through busy London helped solidify my choice to stay and pursue this journey.

In closing I'd like to acknowledge my housemates, Kin 2000. You've become my home away from home. Your energy is endless and a constant source of distraction as well as inspiration. Thank you for keeping me company as I knit late into the night.

Fiona Alice's love of fibre and textiles was sparked at a young age when her mother, Wendy, taught her the basics of knitting. She completed a Bachelor of Fine Arts at the Nova Scotia College of Art and Design in Halifax in 2011. After interning at Toft Alpaca and Pom Pom Quarterly in the UK, she decided to stay indefinitely in London, where she has immersed herself in the knitting community, working at the knitting shop Loop and travelling the country to the many knitting and yarn festivals the UK has to offer. This is her first collection of patterns published as a book. **fionaalice.com**

fiona
alice
halifax knitwear